RENAL DIET

GUIDE FOR THE MANAGEMENT OF KIDNEY DISEASES, WITH FOOD PLAN AND MEAL PLANNING WITH LOW SODIUM, LOW PHOSPHORUS, LOW POTASSIUM AND LIQUID INTAKE.

Table of Contents

Introduction

Renal diet is a dietary regimen designed to bring relief to patients with slow or damaged renal functions and chronic kidney diseases. There is not a single uniformed type of renal diet – this is the case because requirements of renal diet as well as restrictions, need to match the needs of the patient and be based on what doctor prescribed for the patient's overall health.

However, all forms of renal diet have one thing in common, which is to improve your renal functions, bring some relief to your kidneys, as well as prevent kidneys disease at patients with numerous risk factors, altogether improving your overall health and well-being. The grocery list we have provided should help you get ahold of which groceries you should introduce to your diet and which groups of food should be avoided in order to improve your kidneys' performance, so you can start from shopping for your new lifestyle.

You don't need to shop many different types of groceries all at once as it is always better to use fresh produce, although frozen food also makes a good alternative when fresh fruit and vegetables are not available.

As far as the renal diet we are recommending in our guide, this form of kidney-friendly dietary regimen offers solution in form of low-sodium and low-potassium meals and groceries, which is why we are also offering simple and easy renal diet recipes in our guide. By following a dietary plan compiled for all stages of renal system failure unless the doctor recommends a different treatment by allowing or expelling some of the groceries, we have listed in our ultimate grocery list for renal patients.

Before we get to cooking and changing your lifestyle from the very core with the idea of improving your health, we want you to get familiar with renal diet basics and find out exactly what his diet is based on while you already know what is the very core solution found in renal diet – helping you improve your kidney's health by lowering sodium and potassium intake.

The best way of getting familiar with renal diet and basics of this dietary regimen is to take a look at the most commonly asked questions that extend the answer to a question What is renal diet?

What the ingredients are and what they do in a renal diet lifestyle

These are some of the most commonly asked questions that should clarify many of your doubts on what renal diet actually represents and stands for.

What is renal diet based on?

Renal diet is a dietary regimen that restricts food groups that may bring harm to an already damaged renal system and kidneys. The main goal of the diet is to help patients who had already been diagnosed with a form of kidneys disease to live a healthier lifestyle, enabling them to manually regulate presence of sodium, potassium, water and waste that should be otherwise regulated by healthy kidneys and normal renal function. Renal diet is based on introduction of foods that are low in sodium and potassium.

How much protein do I need for normal functions?
Protein requirements and needs may be different from patient to patient, but when talking in general, meat portions should be lowered to minimal consumption, while you may seek for other sources of protein in alternative food options beside meat products such as beef and chicken. Protein is being processed by kidneys and since you are having issues with your renal functions, you need to lower your protein intake. Still, protein consumption should be kept at satisfying levels so your body would be able to function properly. Approximately, in case you are not a dialysis patient, the average protein intake should be anywhere between 0.8 grams of protein per kilogram of your body weight on a daily basis. In case you are a dialysis patient, the average intake of protein per day should be between 1 and 1.3 grams of protein per kilogram of your body weight. In case you have more kilograms than you are supposed to, it is recommended to lose weight in a healthy way with physical activity and healthy diet regimen. Protein helps our body heal in a way, as the presence of protein in our blood called albumin regulates growth as well

as repairment of damaged tissue, which is why protein is important.

Can I use meat substitutes for protein sources?

Patients with kidney disease that dislike or don't consume meat out of different reasons may find a valuable dose of daily protein intake through several alternatives. Even though low protein consumption is recommended when on renal diet, you need to make sure that you are not neglecting the need your body has for protein. That is how renal patients that avoid eating meat need to find ways of taking protein through a daily diet in recommended doses. For instance, instead of meat and in case you can't eat not even small portions of meat, you can turn to animal-based protein found in cheese and eggs. Since only low-sodium and low-potassium cheese is allowed, make sure to find suitable alternatives in case you want to include cheese in your diet. Additionally, you need to talk to your doctor on the quantity of eggs and milk you are allowed to have on a daily and weekly basis. Moreover, you can use egg substitutes and protein shakes mixed with fruit that are suitable for your condition and your diet regimen.

Chapter 1. What's the kidney? What's it for?

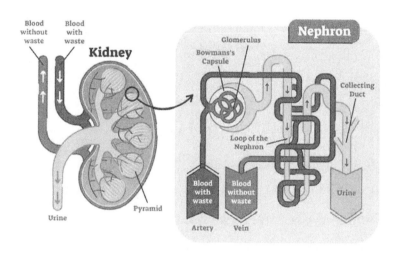

Many people go through their lives, knowing very little about their kidneys. All they know are that they are two medium-sized organs (about the size of an orange) that are shaped similarly to a bean. You may even know that the kidneys are located on each side of your spine, directly below your rib cage. However, this is not enough information about these vital organs. After all, if you don't care for your kidneys, they can become diseased, leading to major health problems.

You will learn all about the importance of your kidneys, how they are constantly sustaining your body, and why you should protect them.

When your kidneys are healthy and capable of actively performing their duties, they will filter an average of four liquid ounces of blood every sixty seconds. While filtering this blood, the kidneys remove extra water which will be made into urine and any waste within the blood. After the water removes the water from the blood, it directs it to the bladder to become urine. This water is transported through the ureters, which are two thin tubes made out of muscle, located on each side of the bladder. This means that your kidneys, along with your bladder and ureters, are all a part of your urinary tract.

Many people mistakenly believe the kidneys act as sponges, which is far from the truth. The kidneys do not absorb and hold onto waste and harmful compounds. Instead, the kidneys filter out these toxins so that they can be completely removed from the body. They do this with a complex system that consists of millions of nephrons, which are microscopic filters. Nephrons are comprised of two components, which are the glomerulus and the tubule. In order to cleanse the blood, the glomerulus strains it of the larger molecules from fluid and waste. After this pass through the glomerulus, they head to the tubule. As the blood travels through the tubule component of the nephrons, smaller molecules of waste are collected. Not only that, but the tubule also collects any minerals found within the blood and then transfers them back into the bloodstream. But, how are these toxins removed from the kidneys and the body so that they don't stay stuck within your organs? When the kidneys filter water from your bloodstream, it combines the water with the filtered waste and toxins, therefore allowing them to be carried to the bladder before being expelled from the body.

Some of the waste that the kidneys remove from your blood is excess acid, which is produced in your blood in order to maintain healthy levels of minerals and water. This acid affects the levels of many minerals, such as potassium, sodium, calcium, and phosphorus. When these minerals are out of balance, your body will be unable to function properly. As these minerals are electrolytes, they affect the maintenance and control of your muscles, nerves, tissues, and balance. Without the proper balance of these electrolytes, you can be in a rather dangerous situation.

Athletes are frequently aware of the importance of maintaining balanced electrolytes, as your body will naturally become depleted of these minerals as you sweat. This is the reason that sports drinks are popular. These drinks contain all the electrolytes the human body requires, allowing people to refuel on both water and minerals simultaneously. However, if you consume too many sports drinks or electrolytes in other forms, you will overload your blood and kidneys. It is important to contain a balance of electrolytes with neither too few nor too many.

Along with filtering out water, maintaining electrolyte levels, and removing excess acid, your kidney provides other functions. This includes the production of red blood cells, blood pressure maintenance, hydration regulation, hormone production, vitamin D production for bone health.

Understanding Kidney Disease

When you educate yourself about chronic kidney disease, you will feel more empowered and less scared about living with the disease. You can take back control of your life! What you eat and the lifestyle choices you make are very important. If you are diagnosed in the early stages of the disease, there are many steps you can take to prolong your kidney function. When you make positive changes, have patience, and commit to working closely with your health-care team, chances are very good that you will be able to enjoy a high-quality, happy, and active life.

What Is Kidney Disease?

Let's begin by understanding how kidneys function. Your body has two kidneys that are bean-shaped and about the size of your fist. When the kidneys are working properly, they help keep your whole body in balance by doing the following very important jobs:

1. Clean waste materials from your blood

2. Remove extra water from your body

3. Regulate your blood pressure

Stimulate your bone marrow to make red blood cells

Control the amount of calcium and phosphorus absorbed and excreted

When you have chronic kidney disease, your kidneys do not work properly and cannot do these jobs. Although there is no cure for kidney failure, it is very possible to live a long and healthy life with proper treatment and good dietary and lifestyle choices.

Causes

Kidney disease is most often caused by poorly controlled diabetes or high blood pressure. Physical injury and drug toxicity can also damage your kidneys. Kidney disease affects people of all ages and races, but African Americans, Hispanics, and Native Americans tend to have a greater risk of kidney failure. This is mostly due to a higher incidence of diabetes and high blood pressure in these populations.

Uncontrolled diabetes is the leading cause of kidney failure. In fact, 44 percent of people who start dialysis have kidney failure caused by diabetes. Diabetes develops when blood glucose (blood sugar) levels are too high in the body. When our bodies digest protein from the food we eat, the process of digestion creates waste products. In the kidneys, millions of small blood vessels, called capillaries, act as filters. As blood flows through the capillaries, the waste products are filtered out into our urine. Substances such as protein and red blood cells are too big to pass through the capillaries and stay in the blood.

Diabetes damages this process. Too much blood is filtered when there is a high levels of blood sugar. All the extra work wears down the filters, and after many years the filters start to leak. The good protein our bodies need is then filtered out and lost through the urine. Eventually, the kidneys cannot remove the extra waste from the blood. This ultimately leads to kidney damage or failure. This damage can happen over many years without any signs or symptoms. That is why it is so important for people with diabetes to manage their blood-sugar levels and get tested for kidney disease periodically.

High blood pressure is another contributor to kidney disease. One in three Americans with high blood pressure, also known as hypertension, is at risk for kidney disease. High blood pressure is the second leading cause of kidney disease and increases your risk of developing a heart attack or stroke. Treatment and lifestyle changes, including blood-pressure medications, following a healthy diet, and exercising can lower blood pressure.

High blood pressure means the heart has to work harder at pumping blood. As time passes, high blood pressure can harm blood vessels in your body, including the ones in your kidneys—which causes them to stop filtering out waste and extra fluid from your body. The extra fluid in your blood vessels can also make your blood pressure rise, creating a vicious and detrimental cycle. As in diabetes, this damage can happen over many years without any signs or symptoms. It is very important for people with high blood pressure to control their blood pressure and get tested for kidney disease, just like people who have diabetes. High blood pressure is the cause of more than 25,000 new cases of kidney failure in the United States every year.

Symptoms

Kidney failure is a progressive disease; it does not happen overnight. Some people in the early stages of kidney disease do not show any symptoms. Symptoms usually appear in the upcoming stages of kidney disease. Some people may not even show any symptoms of kidney disease until their kidneys fail (end stage).

When the kidneys are damaged, wastes and toxins can build up in your body. Once the buildup starts to occur, you may feel sick and experience some of the following symptoms:

- Nausea
- Poor appetite
- Weakness
- Trouble sleeping
- Tiredness
- Itching
- Weight loss
- Muscle cramps (especially in the legs)

- Swelling of your feet and ankles
- Anemia (low red blood cell count)

The good news is that once you begin treatment for kidney disease, your symptoms and general health will start to improve.

Stages Of Chronic Kidney Disease (CKD)

There are five stages of CKD. Each level has a corresponding GFR index that accompanies it. It is very important for someone who has CKD to have continual monitoring of their GFR index because it doesn't take much for the change in the index to trigger the following stage of chronic kidney disease. For this reason alone, it is important to monitor what you are eating in conjunction with your stage of disease.

Stage 1 and 2 CKD (Normal to High and Mild GFR)
Most people who have stage one or two chronic kidney disease do not know that they have it. Their GFR index is generally greater than ninety milliliters per minute for stage one and an index that is sixty to eighty-nine milliliters per minute for stage two. Generally, the people who have been diagnosed with stage one or two CKD were diagnosed because of tests for another illness. Symptoms of stage one and two can be extremely vague, but a good indicator is higher than normal creatinine levels in the blood or urine. With stage two, the filtration levels of the kidney have begun to decrease, but not at an overly noticeable level. People living with stage one and

two CKD can still live a normal life, they can't cure their kidneys, but they can help stop or slow the progression of the disease. Keeping blood pressure in line and eating a diet that is renal friendly are good first steps. Your doctor will keep up on your creatine levels and GFR to monitor the progression of CKD.

Stage 3A and 3B (Moderate GFR)

Stage three is broken up into two GFR indexes, but the symptoms aren't much different. The GFR index for stage A is an index of forty-five to fifty-nine milliliters per minute. The GFR for stage B is thirty to forty-four milliliters per minute. As the kidney's functions decrease, the build-up of wastes causes the body to go into uremia, which is a buildup of that waste in the blood. More complications from kidney failure become apparent. The chances for high blood pressure increase and patients are likely to exhibit anemia. Swelling, or edema, may start to become apparent because of the water retention and typically starts in the arms and legs. Diet becomes increasingly more important with stage three CDK due to the buildup in the body.

Stage 4 (Severe GFR)

Stage four is the last stop before kidney failure. The GFR index for stage four is fifteen to twenty-nine milliliters per minute. Stage four patients are more than likely receiving dialysis and are thinking about transplant in the near future. The body is barely filtering the wastes, hence the mechanical intervention for filtration, edema worsens, and physical symptoms can be overwhelming. Diet in this phase is stricter and will consist of limiting things that can build up in the body that the kidneys are no longer taking care of on their own.

Stage 5 (End Stage GFR)

Once the kidneys are no longer filtering the waste in the body, dialysis will be necessary to live. The GFR index in end-stage is less than fifteen milliliters per minute. There is also a chance that if you meet qualifications, you will be put on a transplant list. Stage five CKD leaves the patient feeling sick almost all of the time because of the toxins and waste built up in the body. A nephrologist, a doctor who specializes in kidneys, will be a permanent part of your medical regimen. Diet will be an absolute must, as will limiting fluid intake.

Chapter 2. Introduction to Power Supply

What To Eat And What To Avoid In Renal Diet

As specified above, some nutrients should be limited in renal diet e.g. phosphorus, potassium, and thus any foods that contain high amounts of these should be taken only in low amounts and not on a daily basis. The foods that should be limited are:

- Bananas

- Avocadoes

- Beetroots

- Dried beans

- Dried fruit

- Mangos

- Melons

- Molasses

- Nuts and seeds

- Oranges

- Parsnips

- Spinach

- Potatoes

- Fish

- Low-fat yogurt

Be attentive! Following foods have a high amount of sodium and their consumption should be limited:

- Salty snacks e.g. pretzels, potato chips, packed popcorn etc.

- Savory pies e.g. cheese pies, sausage rolls, and Greek spinach pies

- Processed meats e.g. luncheon meat, salami, sausages

- Pickled foods in salt brine

- Condiments e.g. ketchup, mustard, and mayo

- Soy sauce

- Canned soups and sauces

Now, here are the top foods you can consume without any (strict) restrictions, as they are naturally low in potassium, phosphorus, and sodium:

- Cabbage

- Cucumber

- Broccoli

- Cauliflower

- Brussels sprouts

- Onions

- Garlic

- Apples

- Berries (blueberries, cranberries, berries, strawberries)

- Cherries

- Red grapes

- Egg whites

- Wild caught fish

- Olive oil

- Bulgur wheat

- Oatmeal

- Skinless chicken and turkey

- Arugula

- Macadamia Nuts

- Radishes

- Shiitake mushrooms

- Pineapple

- Grapefruits

- Kale

- Ginger

- All spices and herbs

Red meat and dairy can also be consumed in moderation, but they should not be combined with high phosphorus, potassium, or sodium foods as they contain moderate amounts of these alone.

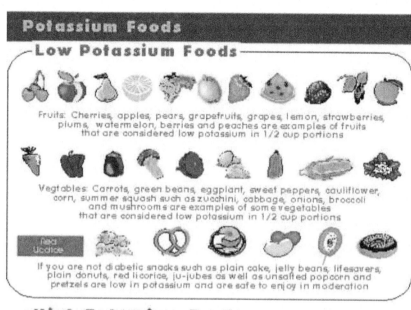

Potassium Foods

Low Potassium Foods

Fruits: Cherries, apples, pears, grapefruits, grapes, lemon, strawberries, plums, watermelon, berries and peaches are examples of fruits that are considered low potassium in 1/2 cup portions

Vegtables: Carrots, green beans, eggplant, sweet peppers, cauliflower, corn, summer squash such as zucchini, cabbage, onions, broccoli and mushrooms are examples of some vegetables that are considered low potassium in 1/2 cup portions

Red Licorice

If you are not diabetic snacks such as plain cake, jelly beans, lifesavers, plain donuts, red licorice, ju-jubes as well as unsalted popcorn and pretzels are low in potassium and are safe to enjoy in moderation

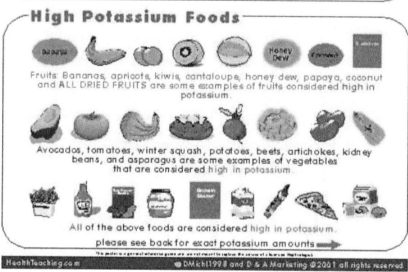

High Potassium Foods

Fruits: Bananas, apricots, kiwis, cantaloupe, honey dew, papaya, coconut and ALL DRIED FRUITS are some examples of fruits considered high in potassium.

Avocados, tomatoes, winter squash, potatoes, beets, artichokes, kidney beans, and asparagus are some examples of vegetables that are considered high in potassium.

All of the above foods are considered high in potassium. please see back for exact potassium amounts ➡

The Benefits Of A Renal Diet

Doctors and dietitians have developed a diet that helps their patients with compromised kidney function cut down the amount of waste that their body produces that their kidneys can't filter out. A renal diet is lower in sodium, phosphorus, and protein than a typical diet. Every person's body is different, which means that what works for one person will not work for another. Some people have to cut their levels of potassium and calcium as well. A renal diet must be tailored to meet the individual needs and toxin levels of the patient. Keeping a food journal may become necessary and is highly recommended. Sometimes it can be hard to keep track of all of the foods and their amounts; a journal can make keeping track a lot less intimidating. A physical notebook or even a cell phone application can be used for this.

Sodium (mg)

Sodium and table salt are two different components. Table salt is comprised of sodium and chloride. However, sodium by itself is a mineral that is naturally occurring in most of the foods that we eat. This is why processed foods are not recommended for someone with kidney problems or in a renal diet due to the added salt that is put into them. Sodium is one of three major electrolytes that help control the fluids going in and out of the cells and tissue in the body. Sodium is responsible for helping control blood pressure and volume, muscle contraction and nerve functions, regulating the acid and base balance of the blood, and balancing the elimination and retention of fluid in the body.

Renal patients are required to monitor their sodium intake because when the kidney's functions become compromised, it is harder for their body to eliminate the fluids and the sodium that is in excess in the body. When it becomes difficult for the body to do this it can cause a number of side effects including:

- Increased thirst
- Edema, which is the swelling of the extremities
- High blood pressure
- Shortness of breath from fluid being retained in the lungs
- Heart failure from an overworked and weak heart that has had to work harder due to the body making it work harder

Limiting sodium can be easier than you think. Since sodium content is always listed on food labels, it is important to get into the habit of checking not only sodium content but the single serving size as well. As a rule of thumb, fresh is better. Packaged foods typically have added salt, so stick with things that have no salt added to them. Start comparing the items you use. If it is a spice, steer clear of something with "salt" in the title. When you are cooking in your home, do not add extra salt to your food under any circumstance. Too much sodium can make chronic kidney disease progress much faster.

Potassium (mg)
Potassium is another of the three major electrolytes in the body. It is a naturally occurring mineral found in many foods and in our own bodies. Potassium helps keep our hearts beating regularly and our muscles working correctly. The

kidneys have a duty when regulating the amount of potassium in the body. These organs, when healthy, know just how much potassium your body needs. Excess potassium is cleansed from the body through the body's urine output. When you have chronic kidney disease, this naturally occurring regulation in the body becomes compromised. High potassium levels in the blood, also known as hyperkalemia, come with the following symptoms:

- Weakness in the muscles
- Irregular heartbeat
- A pulse that is slower than normal
- Heart attack/Stroke
- Death

Learning how to limit potassium, just like sodium, is an important part of your renal diet. Limiting foods that are high in Potassium is your first line of defense when taking on a renal diet. Foods like bananas, fish, spinach, avocados, and potatoes are high in potassium and are foods to avoid. Cut down on your milk and dairy consumption to eight ounces per day. Make sure to read the labels and adhere to the single serving size of the foods you are eating.

Phosphorus (mg)
Phosphorus is a mineral that aids the bones and the muscles in the body. When food is ingested, the small intestines absorb the amount of phosphorus needed for the bones, but the

kidneys are in charge of removing the extra phosphorus. When the kidneys can't expel the extra phosphorus, it builds up in the blood and pulls calcium from the bones, making them weak. High amounts of phosphorus can also cause calcium deposits to build up in the heart, lungs, eyes, and blood vessels.

Keeping phosphorus levels low, just like sodium and potassium, are important in a renal diet. Try to avoid foods that are high in phosphorus like soda, cheese, meat, milk, and seeds. It may be necessary to discuss using phosphate binders with your doctor to keep your levels under control. Make sure you are avoiding foods with added phosphorus. These will be labeled with "PHOS" on the label.

Protein (g)

Protein levels can be a tricky thing to keep equaled out if you have chronic kidney disease. Different stages of CKD tolerate protein levels differently and depending on which stage of CKD you are experiencing; your diet will reflect a different level of proteins allowed. Proteins are important to the body, so you can't eliminate them from your diet. You can be aware of your intake and what your body can tolerate and what it can't.

Fluid

It is important for fluid intake to be strictly monitored due to the probability of the fluid being retained in the body. When a person is on dialysis, their urine output is decreased, so extra fluid can cause unnecessary strain on the body. Fluid intake levels will be calculated by a nutritionist or doctor on a personal basis. Never drink more than what the doctor tells you is okay, and do not forget to consider solids that turn to liquid at room temperature or used in cooking.

Chapter 3. Diet Plan

Meal Planning

THIS WEEK'S MENU   WEEK OF: _____

	MONDAY	TUESDAY	WEDNESDAY	THURSDAY	FRIDAY	SATURDAY	SUNDAY
BREAKFAST							
LUNCH							
DINNER							

NEED TO GET:

Meal planning can make daily life easier all around but can be even more crucial to keeping up with a special diet. Make sure that when you are planning for meals that you leave a little bit of wiggle room for the unexpected schedule change. It is often better to use a small planner or datebook to write down the daily meals you plan on making. This can help you make your grocery list and can help you plan a budget. This can be a time-consuming project when you are first starting out; however, once you get into a routine of doing a meal plan, it can become quite easy.

- Make a list of kidney-friendly breakfasts, lunches, and dinners. Consider what day of the week you will be planning for family dinners, what days you work, etc.
- Plan around current activities and plan only a week at a time to thwart overwhelming yourself and to help budget your meals more effectively.
- Watch sales ads. Most ads come out early enough in the week that you can plan for the following week and use them to their potential.
- Make effective lists. If you are having chicken for dinner on one night but can get a better deal buying a larger quantity, precook the chicken and store it for another meal in the week.

Use your meal planner in conjunction with your food journal. This can help you use your eating habits to make healthier choices. If you prefer something sweet in the evening before bed, swap it out for fruit or something that is friendlier for your diet. If you find yourself snacking at your desk between meals, look into healthier alternatives like a hard candy that might occupy your oral fixation during that time.

Limiting Nutrient Intakes

A dietician or your doctor will be the one who sets limits for your diet and the amount you should be consuming every day. Included are the limits for a typical renal diet. These are the amounts that may be higher or lower than the ones assigned to you, but they reflect the standard renal diet.

Phosphorus (mg)

Phosphorus is generally limited to 1000 milligrams a day. Generally, a doctor will prescribe a phosphate binder to take with your meals. Foods high in phosphorus dark-colored sodas.

Potassium

Potassium should be limited to 2000 milligrams a day. Foods that are high in potassium are bananas, avocados, melons, and black beans.

Sodium (mg)

Sodium intake amounts can vary, as a general rule of thumb, 2000 milligrams is typically the limit for renal diet patients. Sodium is something that is found in most foods and is a natural substance, so the best advice to take is "no added salt." Try using regular herbs in place of salting food. Salt substitutes also tend to be high in potassium, but if you are under on your potassium intake, they can be a nice alternative.

Protein (g)

Protein has an important role in the body. It fuels the body and helps it fight infections. Limiting protein consumption to only seven or eight ounces a day can help keep the body functioning but protect the kidneys from receiving too much.

Being Successful

Moderation is the key to any successful diet or lifestyle. Dietary guidelines promote eating all kinds of food, as long as they are enjoyed in moderation. This also holds true for a renal diet. You don't have to give up all the things that you love; you just have to monitor how much and how often you enjoy them. Keys to make the lifestyle change work are:

- Slow down while you are eating. It takes the body almost twenty minutes to send the signal to the brain that it is full. This is how people overeat, they eat too quickly, and the brain can't catch up until it is too late.

- Stop eating when you become full. It is okay to walk away from the table, feeling like you could eat more. Let your body tell you when it has had enough.

- Eat the cake but make it a small piece. Enjoy every bite, taste, and sensation of that piece of cake.

- If you are eating a large helping of something, especially in a restaurant, enjoy it. Eat half of it then and then take the rest home and enjoy it again the following day.

- You can reward yourself. Do it in moderation, though. Know what your body can and can't handle and use your food journal to alert you on where your levels stand for the day. It isn't just a tool, but more of an ally and best friend.

The goal of keeping track of everything is to turn the renal diet lifestyle into a marathon instead of a race. Keeping up with a lifestyle change that will be a permanent part of your life will be more encouraging than trying a short-term diet that can actually become psychologically harmful to your health.

Diet Plan

DAY	BREAKFAST	LUNCH	DINNER	SNACK/DESSERT
1	MOZZARELLA CHEESE OMELETTE	BAKED CAULIFLOWER AND BROCCOLI MAC AND CHEESE	PORK CHILI	BUFFALO CAULIFLOWER BITES WITH DAIRY FREE RANCH DRESSING
2	SUN-DRIED TOMATO FRITTATA	CARAWAY CABBAGE AND RICE	GROUND PORK WITH WATER CHESTNUTS	PHILLY CHEESESTEAK STUFFED MUSHROOMS
3	ITALIAN BREAKFAST FRITTATA	GRATIN PASTA WITH WATERCRESS AND CHICKEN	GLAZED PORK CHOPS WITH PEACH	GREEK COOKIES
4	SAUSAGE CHEESE BAKE OMELETTE	ORZO AND VEGETABLES	PORK CHOPS IN CREAMY SAUCE	HAM AND DILL PICKLE BITES
5	GREEK EGG SCRAMBLED	LEMON RICE WITH	BAKED PORK & MUSHROO	EASY FLAVORED POTATOES MIX

		VEGETABLES	M MEATBALLS	
6	FETA MINT OMELETTE	CHICKEN AND ASPARAGUS PASTA	BUTTERNUT SQUASH, KALE AND GROUND BEEF BREAKFAST BOWL	EGGPLANT SANDWICH
7	SAUSAGE BREAKFAST CASSEROLE	HAWAIIAN RICE	LIGHT BEEF SOUP	NO BAKE OAT COOKIES
8	EASY TURNIP PUREE	MEXICAN RICE	BEEF NOODLE SOUP	CHOCOLATE COCONUT QUINOA SLICES
9	SPINACH BACON BREAKFAST BAKE	SHRIMP FRIED RICE	SPANISH RICE CASSEROLE WITH BEEF	APPLE AND NUT CHEWS
10	HEALTHY SPINACH TOMATO MUFFINS	VEGETARIAN EGG FRIED RICE	KEFTA STYLED BEEF PATTIES WITH CUCUMBER SALAD	BANANA CAROB BARS WITH A CHILI TWIST
11	CHICKEN EGG BREAKFAST MUFFINS	AUTUMN ORZO SALAD	BROILED LAMB SHOULDER	LEMON MOUSSE
12	VEGETABLE TOFU SCRAMBLE	BLACKENED SHRIMP AND PINEAPPLE SALAD	PAN-SEARED LAMB CHOPS	JALAPENO CRISP

13	KETO OVERNIGHT OATS	GREEN PEPPER SLAW	ROASTED LAMB CHOPS WITH RELISH	RASPBERRY POPSICLE
14	CHEESE COCONUT PANCAKES	ITALIAN CHICKEN SALAD	GRILLED LAMB CHOPS	EASY FUDGE
15	COCONUT BREAKFAST SMOOTHIE	CRANBERRIES AND COUSCOUS SALAD	LAMB BURGERS WITH AVOCADO DIP	BLUEBERRY MUFFINS
16	CINNAMON CHEESE PANCAKES	TUNA SALAD	LAMB & PINEAPPLE KEBABS	THE COCONUT LOAF
17	BREAKFAST EGG SALAD	MIXED BERRY AND FRUIT SALAD	BAKED MEATBALLS & SCALLIONS	CHOCOLATE PARFAIT
18	CREAMY CINNAMON SCRAMBLED EGG	ROASTED VEGETABLE SALAD	PORK WITH BELL PEPPER	CAULIFLOWER BAGEL
19	CHOCO COCONUT SMOOTHIE	CHICKEN PITA PIZZA	PORK WITH PINEAPPLE	ALMOND CRACKERS
20	HEALTHY CHIA PUDDING	CAULIFLOWER STEAK SANDWICHES	SPICED PORK	CASHEW AND ALMOND BUTTER
21	CHEESY SCRAMBLED EGGS WITH FRESH HERBS	SALAD WITH VINAIGRETTE	GRILLED SPICED TURKEY	BASIC MEAT LOAF

22	TURKEY AND SPINACH SCRAMBLE ON MELBA TOAST	SALAD WITH LEMON DRESSING	HERBY CHICKEN STEW	CEREAL MUNCH
23	VEGETABLE OMELET	SHRIMP WITH SALSA	LEMON & HERB CHICKEN WRAPS	COCONUT MANDARIN SALAD
24	MEXICAN STYLE BURRITOS	CAULIFLO WER SOUP	GINGER & BEAN SPROUT STEAK STIR-FRY	CREAM DIPPED CUCUMBERS
25	BLUEBERRY MUFFINS	CABBAGE STEW	CARROT & GINGER CHICKEN NOODLES	BARBECUE CUPS
26	BULGUR, COUSCOUS AND BUCKWHEAT CEREAL	BAKED HADDOCK	ROAST BEEF	SPICED PRETZELS
27	SWEET PANCAKES	HERBED CHICKEN	BEEF BROCHETT ES	CAULIFLOWER WITH MUSTARD SAUCE
28	BREAKFAST SMOOTHIE	PESTO PORK CHOPS	COUNTRY FRIED STEAK	PINEAPPLE CABBAGE COLESLAW

Chapter 4. Recipes (Breakfast, Lunch, Dinner and Snacks)

Breakfast Recipes

Mozzarella Cheese Omelette

Preparation Time: 10 minutes
Cooking Time: 5 minutes
Servings: 1
Ingredients:
4 eggs, beaten
1/4 cup mozzarella cheese, shredded
4 tomato slices
1/4 tsp Italian seasoning
1/4 tsp dried oregano
Pepper
Salt
Directions:
In a small bowl, whisk eggs with salt.
Spray pan with cooking spray and heat over medium heat.
Pour egg mixture into the pan and cook over medium heat.
Once eggs are set then sprinkle oregano and Italian seasoning on top.
Arrange tomato slices on top of the omelet and sprinkle with shredded cheese.
Cook omelet for 1 minute.
Serve and enjoy.
Nutrition:
Calories 285
Fat 19 g
Carbohydrates 4g
Protein 25 g

Sun-Dried Tomato Frittata

Preparation Time: 10 minutes
Cooking Time: 20 minutes
Servings: 8
Ingredients:

12 eggs

1/2 tsp dried basil

1/4 cup parmesan cheese, grated

2 cups baby spinach, shredded

1/4 cup sun-dried tomatoes, sliced

Pepper

Salt

Directions:

Preheat the oven to 425 F.

In a large bowl, whisk eggs with pepper and salt.

Add remaining ingredients and stir to combine.

Spray oven-safe pan with cooking spray.

Pour egg mixture into the pan and bake for 20 minutes.

Slice and serve.

Nutrition:

Calories 115

Fat 7 g

Carbohydrates 1 g

Protein 10 g

Italian Breakfast Frittata

Preparation Time: 10 minutes
Cooking Time: 45 minutes
Servings: 4
Ingredients:
2 cups egg whites
1/2 cup mozzarella cheese, shredded
1 cup cottage cheese, crumbled
1/4 cup fresh basil, sliced
1/2 cup roasted red peppers, sliced
Pepper
Salt
Directions:
Preheat the oven to 375 F.
Add all ingredients into the large bowl and whisk well to combine.
Pour frittata mixture into the baking dish and bake for 45 minutes.
Slice and serve.
Nutrition:
Calories 131
Fat 2 g
Carbohydrates 5 g
Protein 22 g

Sausage Cheese Bake Omelette

Preparation Time: 10 minutes
Cooking Time: 45 minutes
Servings: 8
Ingredients:

16 eggs

2 cups cheddar cheese, shredded

1/2 cup salsa

1 lb ground sausage

1 1/2 cups coconut milk

Pepper

Salt

Directions:

Preheat the oven to 350 F.

Add sausage in a pan and cook until browned. Drain excess fat.

In a large bowl, whisk eggs and milk. Stir in cheese, cooked sausage, and salsa.

Pour omelet mixture into the baking dish and bake for 45 minutes.

Serve and enjoy.

Nutrition:

Calories 360

Fat 24 g

Carbohydrates 4 g

Protein 28 g

Greek Egg Scrambled

Preparation Time: 10 minutes
Cooking Time: 10 minutes
Servings: 2
Ingredients:

4 eggs

1/2 cup grape tomatoes, sliced

2 tbsp green onions, sliced

1 bell pepper, diced

1 tbsp olive oil

1/4 tsp dried oregano

1/2 tbsp capers

3 olives, sliced

Pepper

Salt

Directions:

Heat oil in a pan over medium heat.

Add green onions and bell pepper and cook until pepper is softened.

Add tomatoes, capers, and olives and cook for 1 minute.

Add eggs and stir until eggs are cooked. Season with oregano, pepper, and salt.

Serve and enjoy.

Nutrition:

Calories 230

Fat 17 g

Carbohydrates 8 g

Protein 12 g

Feta Mint Omelette

Preparation Time: 10 minutes
Cooking Time: 5 minutes
Servings: 1
Ingredients:

3 eggs
1/4 cup fresh mint, chopped
2 tbsp coconut milk
1/2 tsp olive oil
2 tbsp feta cheese, crumbled
Pepper
Salt

Directions:

In a bowl, whisk eggs with feta cheese, mint, milk, pepper, and salt.
Heat olive oil in a pan over low heat.
Pour egg mixture in the pan and cook until eggs are set.
Flip omelet and cook for 2 minutes more.
Serve and enjoy.

Nutrition:

Calories 275
Fat 20 g
Carbohydrates 4 g
Protein 20 g

Sausage Breakfast Casserole

Preparation Time: 10 minutes
Cooking Time: 50 minutes
Servings: 8
Ingredients:

12 eggs

1 lb. ground Italian sausage

2 1/2 tomatoes, sliced

3 tbsp coconut flour

1/4 cup coconut milk

2 small zucchinis, shredded

Pepper

Salt

Directions:

Preheat the oven to 350 F.

Spray casserole dish with cooking spray and set aside.

Cook sausage in a pan until brown.

Transfer sausage to a mixing bowl.

Add coconut flour, milk, eggs, zucchini, pepper, and salt. Stir well.

Add eggs and whisk to combine.

Transfer bowl mixture into the casserole dish and top with tomato slices.

Bake for 50 minutes.

Serve and enjoy.

Nutrition:

Calories 305

Fat 21.8 g

Carbohydrates 6.3 g

Protein 19.6 g

Easy Turnip Puree

Preparation Time: 10 minutes
Cooking Time: 12 minutes
Servings: 4
Ingredients:

1 1/2 lbs. turnips, peeled and chopped

1 tsp dill

3 bacon slices, cooked and chopped

2 tbsp fresh chives, chopped

Directions:

Add turnip into the boiling water and cook for 12 minutes. Drain well and place in a food processor.

Add dill and process until smooth.

Transfer turnip puree into the bowl and top with bacon and chives.

Serve and enjoy.

Nutrition:

Calories 127

Fat 6 g

Carbohydrates 11.6 g

Protein 6.8 g

Spinach Bacon Breakfast Bake

Preparation Time: 10 minutes
Cooking Time: 45 minutes
Servings: 6
Ingredients:

10 eggs

3 cups baby spinach, chopped

1 tbsp olive oil

8 bacon slices, cooked and chopped

2 tomatoes, sliced

2 tbsp chives, chopped

Pepper

Salt

Directions:

Preheat the oven to 350 F.

Spray a baking dish with cooking spray and set aside.

Heat oil in a pan.

Add spinach and cook until spinach wilted.

In a mixing bowl, whisk eggs and salt. Add spinach and chives and stir well.

Pour egg mixture into the baking dish.

Top with tomatoes and bacon and bake for 45 minutes.

Serve and enjoy.

Nutrition:

Calories 273

Fat 20.4 g

Carbohydrates 3.1 g

Protein 19.4 g

Healthy Spinach Tomato Muffins

Preparation Time: 10 minutes

Cooking Time: 20 minutes

Servings: 12

Ingredients:

12 eggs

1/2 tsp Italian seasoning

1 cup tomatoes, chopped

4 tbsp water

1 cup fresh spinach, chopped

Pepper

Salt

Directions:

Preheat the oven to 350 F.

Spray a muffin tray with cooking spray and set aside.

In a mixing bowl, whisk eggs with water, Italian seasoning, pepper, and salt.

Add spinach and tomatoes and stir well.

Pour egg mixture into the prepared muffin tray and bake for 20 minutes.

Serve and enjoy.

Nutrition:

Calories 67

Fat 4.5 g

Carbohydrates 1 g

Protein 5.7 g

Chicken Egg Breakfast Muffins

Preparation Time: 10 minutes
Cooking Time: 15 minutes
Servings: 12
Ingredients:

10 eggs

1 cup cooked chicken, chopped

3 tbsp green onions, chopped

1/4 tsp garlic powder

Pepper

Salt

Directions:

Preheat the oven to 400 F.

Spray a muffin tray with cooking spray and set aside.

In a large bowl, whisk eggs with garlic powder, pepper, and salt.

Add remaining ingredients and stir well.

Pour egg mixture into the muffin tray and bake for 15 minutes.

Serve and enjoy.

Nutrition:

Calories 71

Fat 4 g

Carbohydrates 0.4 g

Protein 8 g

Vegetable Tofu Scramble

Preparation Time: 10 minutes
Cooking Time: 7 minutes
Servings: 2
Ingredients:
1/2 block firm tofu, crumbled
1/4 tsp ground cumin
1 tbsp turmeric
1 cup spinach
1/4 cup zucchini, chopped
1 tbsp olive oil
1 tomato, chopped
1 tbsp chives, chopped
1 tbsp coriander, chopped
Pepper
Salt
Directions:
Heat oil in a pan over medium heat.
Add tomato, zucchini, and spinach and sauté for 2 minutes.
Add tofu, cumin, turmeric, pepper, and salt and sauté for 5 minutes.
Top with chives, and coriander.
Serve and enjoy.
Nutrition:
Calories 101
Fat 8.5 g
Carbohydrates 5.1 g
Protein 3.1 g

Keto Overnight Oats

Preparation Time: 5 minutes
Cooking Time: 5 minutes
Servings: 2
Ingredients:
1 tbsp chia seed
4 drops liquid stevia
1/2 cup hemp hearts
2/3 cup coconut milk
1/2 tsp vanilla
Pinch of salt
Directions:
Add all ingredients into the bowl and mix well.
Cover and place in refrigerator for 8 hours.
Serve and enjoy.
Nutrition:
Calories 289
Fat 22.5 g
Carbohydrates 5 g
Protein 14 g

Cheese Coconut Pancakes

Preparation Time: 10 minutes
Cooking Time: 5 minutes
Servings: 1
Ingredients:

2 eggs

1 packet stevia

1/2 tsp cinnamon

2 oz cream cheese

1 tbsp coconut flour

1/2 tsp vanilla

Directions:

Add all ingredients into the bowl and blend until smooth.

Spray pan with cooking spray and heat over medium-high heat.

Pour batter on the hot pan and make two pancakes.

Cook pancake until lightly brown from both the sides.

Serve and enjoy.

Nutrition:
Calories 386
Fat 30 g
Carbohydrates 12 g
Protein 16 g

Coconut Breakfast Smoothie

Preparation Time: 5 minutes
Cooking Time: 5 minutes
Servings: 1
Ingredients:
1/4 cup whey protein powder
1/2 cup coconut milk
5 drops liquid stevia
1 tbsp coconut oil
1 tsp vanilla
2 tbsp coconut butter
1/4 cup water
1/2 cup ice
Directions:
Add all ingredients into the blender and blend until smooth.
Serve and enjoy.
Nutrition:
Calories 560
Fat 45 g
Carbohydrates 12 g
Protein 25 g

Cinnamon Cheese Pancakes

Preparation Time: 10 minutes
Cooking Time: 10 minutes
Servings: 4
Ingredients:

4 eggs

1/2 cup cream cheese

1/2 cup almond flour

1 tbsp butter, melted

1/2 tsp cinnamon

Directions:

Add all ingredients except butter into the blender and blend until well combined.

The heat melted butter in a pan over medium heat.

Pour 3 tbsp of batter on the pan and make pancakes and cook for 2 minutes on each side.

Serve and enjoy.

Nutrition:

Calories 271

Fat 24 g

Carbohydrates 4 g

Protein 10 g

Breakfast Egg Salad

Preparation Time: 10 minutes
Cooking Time: 5 minutes
Servings: 4
Ingredients:
6 eggs, hard-boiled, peeled and chopped
1/2 cup dill pickles, chopped
1 tbsp fresh dill, chopped
4 tbsp mayonnaise
Pepper
Salt
Directions:
Add all ingredients into the large bowl and stir to mix.
Serve and enjoy.
Nutrition:
Calories 140
Fat 10 g
Carbohydrates 4 g
Protein 8 g

Creamy Cinnamon Scrambled Egg

Preparation Time: 10 minutes
Cooking Time: 5 minutes
Servings: 2
Ingredients:

4 eggs

1/4 tsp ground cinnamon

2 tbsp heavy cream

1 tbsp butter

Pepper

Salt

Directions:

In a bowl, whisk together eggs and heavy cream.

Melt butter in a pan over medium heat.

Add the egg mixture in a pan and stir until eggs are cooked. Remove pan from heat.

Sprinkle with ground cinnamon.

Serve and enjoy.

Nutrition:

Calories 186

Fat 15 g

Carbohydrates 1 g

Protein 12 g

Choco Coconut Smoothie

Preparation Time: 5 minutes

Cooking Time: 5 minutes

Servings: 1

Ingredients:

1/2 tbsp cocoa powder

1/4 cup heavy cream

5 drops liquid stevia

1/4 cup coconut milk

1/2 cup unsweetened almond milk

Directions:

Add all ingredients to the blender and blend until smooth.
Serve and enjoy.

Nutrition:

Calories 201

Fat 19 g

Carbohydrates 7 g

Protein 2 g

Healthy Chia Pudding

Preparation Time: 5 minutes

Cooking Time: 5 minutes

Servings: 1

Ingredients:

2 tbsp chia seeds

2 strawberries, sliced

1/2 cup unsweetened coconut milk

Directions:

Add coconut milk and chia seeds into a serving bowl and stir well.

Top with sliced strawberries and serve.

Nutrition:

Calories 125

Fat 11 g

Carbohydrates 9 g

Protein 4 g

Cheesy Scrambled Eggs With Fresh Herbs

Preparation Time: 15 minutes
Cooking Time: 10 minutes
Servings: 4

Ingredients

Eggs – 3

Egg whites – 2

Cream cheese – ½ cup

Unsweetened rice milk – ¼ cup

Chopped scallion – 1 Tbsp. green part only

Chopped fresh tarragon – 1 Tbsp.

Unsalted butter – 2 Tbsps.

Ground black pepper to taste

Directions:

In a bowl, whisk the eggs, egg whites, cream cheese, rice milk, scallions, and tarragon until mixed and smooth.

Melt the butter in a skillet.

Pour in the egg mixture and cook, stirring, for 5 minutes or until the eggs are thick and curds creamy.

Season with pepper and serve.

Nutrition:

Calories: 221

Fat: 19g

Carb: 3g

Phosphorus: 119mg

Potassium: 140mg

Sodium: 193mg

Protein: 8g

Turkey And Spinach Scramble On Melba Toast

Preparation Time: 2 minutes

Cooking Time: 15 minutes

Servings: 2

Ingredients

Extra virgin olive oil – 1 tsp

Raw spinach – 1 cup

Garlic – ½ clove, minced

Nutmeg – 1 tsp. grated

Cooked and diced turkey breast – 1 cup

Melba toast – 4 slices

Balsamic vinegar – 1 tsp.

Directions:

Heat a skillet over medium heat and add oil.

Add turkey and heat through for 6 to 8 minutes.

Add spinach, garlic, and nutmeg and stir-fry for 6 minutes more.

Plate up the Melba toast and top with spinach and turkey scramble.

Drizzle with balsamic vinegar and serve.

Nutrition:

Calories: 301

Fat: 19g

Carb: 12g

Phosphorus: 215mg

Potassium: 269mg

Sodium: 360mg

Protein: 19g

Vegetable Omelet

Preparation Time: 15 minutes
Cooking Time: 10 minutes
Servings: 3
Ingredients
Egg whites – 4
Egg – 1
Chopped fresh parsley – 2 Tbsps.
Water – 2 Tbsps.
Olive oil spray
Chopped and boiled red bell pepper – ½ cup
Chopped scallion – ¼ cup, both green and white parts
Ground black pepper

Directions:

Whisk together the egg, egg whites, parsley, and water until well blended. Set aside.

Spray a skillet with olive oil spray and place over medium heat.

Sauté the peppers and scallion for 3 minutes or until softened.

Pour the egg mixture into the skillet over vegetables and cook, swirling the skillet, for 2 minutes or until the edges start to set. Cook until set.

Season with black pepper and serve.

Nutrition:

Calories: 77
Fat: 3g
Carb: 2g
Phosphorus: 67mg
Potassium: 194mg
Sodium: 229mg
Protein: 12g

Mexican Style Burritos

Preparation Time: 5 minutes

Cooking Time: 15 minutes

Servings: 2

Ingredients

Olive oil – 1 Tbsp.

Corn tortillas – 2

Red onion – ¼ cup, chopped

Red bell peppers – ¼ cup, chopped

Red chili – ½, deseeded and chopped

Eggs – 2

Juice of 1 lime

Cilantro – 1 Tbsp. chopped

Directions:

Turn the broiler to medium heat and place the tortillas underneath for 1 to 2 minutes on each side or until lightly toasted.

Remove and keep the broiler on.

Heat the oil in a skillet and sauté onion, chili and bell peppers for 5 to 6 minutes or until soft.

Crack the eggs over the top of the onions and peppers and place skillet under the broiler for 5 to 6 minutes or until the eggs are cooked.

Serve half the eggs and vegetables on top of each tortilla and sprinkle with cilantro and lime juice to serve.

Nutrition:

Calories: 202

Fat: 13g

Carb: 19g

Phosphorus: 184mg

Potassium: 233mg

Sodium: 77mg

Protein: 9g

Blueberry Muffins

Preparation Time: 15 minutes
Cooking Time: 30 minutes
Servings: 12

Ingredients

Unsweetened rice milk – 2 cups

Apple cider vinegar – 1 Tbsp.

All-purpose flour – 3 ½ cups

Granulated sugar – 1 cup

Baking soda substitute – 1 Tbsp.

Ground cinnamon – 1 tsp.

Ground nutmeg – ½ tsp.

Pinch ground ginger

Canola oil – ½ cup

Pure vanilla extract – 2 Tbsps.

Fresh blueberries – 2 ½ cups

Directions:

Preheat the oven to 375F.

Line the cups of a muffin pan with paper liners. Set aside.

In a small bowl, stir together the rice milk and vinegar. Set aside for 10 minutes.

In a large bowl, stir together the sugar, flour, baking soda, cinnamon, nutmeg, and ginger until well mixed.

Add the oil and vanilla to the milk mixture and stir to blend.

Add the milk mixture to the dry ingredients and stir until just combined.

Fold in the blueberries. Spoon the muffin batter evenly into the cups.

Bake the muffins for 25 to 30 minutes or until golden and a toothpick inserted comes out clean.

Cool for 15 minutes and serve.

Nutrition:
Calories: 331
Fat: 11g
Carb: 52g
Phosphorus: 90mg
Potassium: 89mg
Sodium: 35mg
Protein: 6g

Bulgur, Couscous And Buckwheat Cereal

Preparation Time: 10 minutes
Cooking Time: 25 minutes
Servings: 4
Ingredients
Water – 2 ¼ cups
Vanilla rice milk – 1 ¼ cups
Uncooked bulgur – 6 Tbsps.
Uncooked whole buckwheat – 2 Tbsps.
Sliced apple – 1 cup
Plain uncooked couscous – 6 Tbsps.
Ground cinnamon – ½ tsp.

Directions:

In a saucepan, heat the water and milk over medium heat.

Bring to a boil, and add the bulgur, buckwheat, and apple.

Reduce the heat to low and simmer, occasionally stirring until the bulgur is tender, about 20 to 25 minutes.

Remove the saucepan from the heat and stir in the couscous and cinnamon.

Let the saucepan stand, covered, for 10 minutes.

Fluff the cereal with a fork before serving.

Nutrition:

Calories: 159
Fat: 1g
Carb: 34g
Phosphorus: 130mg
Potassium: 116mg
Sodium: 33mg
Protein: 4g

Sweet Pancakes

Preparation Time: 10 minutes
Cooking Time: 5 minutes
Servings: 5
Ingredients
All-purpose flour – 1 cup
Granulated sugar – 1 Tbsp.
Baking powder – 2 tsps.
Egg whites – 2
Almond milk - 1 cup
Olive oil - 2 Tbsps.
Maple extract – 1 Tbsp.

Directions:

Mix the flour, sugar and baking powder in a bowl.

Make a well in the center and place to one side.

In another bowl, mix the egg whites, milk, oil, and maple extract.

Add the egg mixture to the well and gently mix until a batter is formed.

Heat skillet over medium heat.

Add 1/5 of the batter to the pan and cook 2 minutes on each side or until the pancake is golden.

Repeat with the remaining batter and serve.

Nutrition:

Calories: 178
Fat: 6g
Carb: 25g
Phosphorus: 116mg
Potassium: 126mg
Sodium: 297mg
Protein: 6g

Breakfast Smoothie

Preparation Time: 15 minutes
Cooking Time: 0 minutes
Servings: 2

Ingredients

Frozen blueberries – 1 cup

Pineapple chunks – ½ cup

English cucumber – ½ cup

Apple – ½

Water – ½ cup

Directions:

Put the pineapple, blueberries, cucumber, apple, and water in a blender and blend until thick and smooth.

Pour into 2 glasses and serve.

Nutrition:

Calories: 87

Fat: g

Carb: 22g

Phosphorus: 28mg

Potassium: 192mg

Sodium: 3mg

Protein: 0.7g

Buckwheat And Grapefruit Porridge

Preparation Time: 5 minutes
Cooking Time: 20 minutes
Servings: 2

Ingredients

Buckwheat – ½ cup

Grapefruit – ¼, chopped

Honey – 1 Tbsp.

Almond milk – 1 ½ cups

Water – 2 cups

Directions:

Bring the water to a boil on the stove. Add the buckwheat and place the lid on the pan.

Lower heat slightly and simmer for 7 to 10 minutes, checking to ensure water does not dry out.

When most of the water is absorbed, remove and set aside for 5 minutes.

Drain any excess water from the pan and stir in almond milk, heating through for 5 minutes.

Add the honey and grapefruit.

Serve.

Nutrition:

Calories: 231

Fat: 4g

Carb: 43g

Phosphorus: 165mg

Potassium: 370mg

Sodium: 135mg

Egg And Veggie Muffins

Preparation Time: 15 minutes
Cooking Time: 20 minutes
Servings: 4
Ingredients
Cooking spray
Eggs – 4
Unsweetened rice milk – 2 Tbsp.
Sweet onion – ½, chopped
Red bell pepper – ½, chopped
Pinch red pepper flakes
Pinch ground black pepper

Directions:
Preheat the oven to 350F.
Spray 4 muffin pans with cooking spray. Set aside.
In a bowl, whisk together the milk, eggs, onion, red pepper, parsley, red pepper flakes, and black pepper until mixed.
Pour the egg mixture into prepared muffin pans.
Bake until the muffins are puffed and golden, about 18 to 20 minutes.
serve

Nutrition:
Calories: 84
Fat: 5g
Carb: 3g
Phosphorus: 110mg
Potassium: 117mg
Sodium: 75mg
Protein: 7g

Poached Asparagus And Egg

Preparation Time: 3 minutes
Cooking Time: 15 minutes
Servings:1
Ingredients:

1 egg

4 spears asparagus

Water

Directions:

Half-fill a deep saucepan with water set over high heat. Let the water come to a boil.

Dip asparagus spears in water. Cook until they turn a shade brighter, about 3 minutes. Remove from saucepan and drain on paper towels. Keep warm. Lightly season prior to serving.

Using a slotted spoon, gently lower egg into boiling water. Cook for only 4 minutes. Remove from pan immediately. Place on egg holder.

Slice off the top. The egg should still be fluid inside.

Place asparagus spears on a small plate and serve egg on the side. Dip asparagus into the egg and eat while warm.

Nutrition:

Calories 178, Carbs 1g, Fat 13g, Protein 7.72g

Apple Turnover

Preparation Time: 10 minutes
Cooking Time: 15 minutes
Servings:8
Ingredients:
For the turnovers:
½ tsp. cinnamon powder
All-purpose flour
½ cup unwashed palm sugar
1 tbsp. almond flour
1 frozen puff pastry
4 peeled, cored and diced baking apples.
For the egg wash:
2 tbsps. Water
1 whisked egg white

Directions:
To make the filling: combine almond flour, cinnamon powder and palm sugar until these resemble coarse meal. Toss in diced apples until well coated. Set aside.

On a lightly floured surface, roll out the puff pastry until ¼ inch thin. Slice into 8 pieces of 4" x 4" squares.

Divide the prepared apples into 8 equal portions. Spoon on individual puff pastry squares. Fold in half diagonally. Press edges to seal.

Place each filled pastry on a baking tray lined with parchment paper. Make sure there is ample space between pastries.

Freeze for at least 20 minutes, or until ready to bake.

Preheat oven to 400°F for 10 minutes.

Brush frozen pastries with egg wash. Place in the hot oven, and cook for 12 to 15 minutes, or until they turn golden brown all over.

Remove baking tray from oven immediately. Cool slightly for easier handling.

Place 1 apple turnover on a plate. Serve warm.
Nutrition:
Protein 3.81g Carbs 35.75g, Calories 285, Fat 14.78g

Egg Drop Soup

Preparation Time: 5 minutes

Cooking Time: 10 minutes

Servings:4

Ingredients:

¼ cup minced fresh chives

4 cups unsalted vegetable stock

4 whisked eggs

Directions:

Pour unsalted vegetable stock into the oven set over high heat. Bring to a boil. Turn down heat to the lowest heat setting.

Pour in the eggs. Stir continuously until ribbons form into the soup.

Turn off the heat immediately. The residual heat will cook eggs through.

Cool slightly before ladling the desired amount into individual bowls. Garnish with a pinch of parsley, if using. Serve immediately.

Nutrition:

Calories 32, Carbs 0g, Fat 2 g, Protein 5.57g

Summer Squash And Apple Soup

Preparation Time: 10 minutes
Cooking Time: 40 minutes
Servings:4
Ingredients:

1 cup non-dairy milk

½ tsp. cumin

3 cups unsalted vegetable broth

1 ½ tsps. Grated ginger

1 tbsp. olive oil

1 lb. peeled summer squash

2 diced apples

¾ tsp. curry powder

Directions:

Set the oven to 375 °F.

Cut out a sheet of aluminum foil that is big enough to wrap the summer squash. Once wrapped, bake for 30 minutes.

Remove the wrapped summer squash from the oven and set aside to cool.

Once cooled, remove the aluminum foil, remove the seeds, and peel.

Dice the summer squash, then place in a food processor. Add non-dairy milk. Blend until smooth. Transfer to a bowl and set aside.

Place a soup pot over medium flame and heat through. Once hot, add the olive oil and swirl to coat.

Sauté the onion until tender, then add the diced apple, spices, and broth. Bring to a boil. Once boiling, reduce to a simmer and let simmer for about 8 minutes.

Turn off the heat and let cool slightly. Once cooled, pour the mixture into the food processor and blend until smooth.

Pour the pureed apple mixture back into the pot, then stir in the summer squash mixture. Mix well, then reheat to a simmer over medium flame. Serve.

Nutrition:

Calories 240, Protein 2.24g, Fat 8g, Carbs 40g

Roasted Pepper Soup

Preparation Time: 10 minutes

Cooking Time: 30 minutes

Servings:4

Ingredients:

2 cups unsalted vegetable broth

½ cup chopped carrots

2 large red peppers

¼ cup julienned sweet basil

2 minced garlic cloves

½ cup chopped celery

2 tbsps. Olive oil

½ cup chopped onion

½ cup almond milk

Directions:

Place the oven into the 375°F.

Put onions on a baking sheet. Add the red peppers beside the mixture. Drizzle some of the olive oil over everything and toss well to coat.

Roast for 20 minutes, or until peppers are tender and skins are wilted.

Chop the roasted red peppers and set aside.

Place a pot over medium high flame and heat through. Once hot, add the olive oil and swirl to coat.

Place the carrot, celery, and garlic into the pot and sauté until carrot and celery are tender. Add the chopped roasted red peppers. Mix well.

Pour in the vegetable broth and almond milk. Increase to high flame and bring to a boil.

Once boiling, reduce to a simmer. Simmer, uncovered, for 10 minutes.

Turn off the heat and allow to cool slightly.

If desired, blend the soup using an immersion blender until the soup has reached a desired level of smoothness. Reheat over medium flame.

Add the basil and stir to combine. Serve.

Nutrition:

Calories 320, Protein 1.3g, Fat 25g, Carbs 20g

Snack And Dessert Recipes

Buffalo Cauliflower Bites With Dairy Free Ranch Dressing

Preparation Time: 15 minutes
Cooking Time: 30 minutes
Servings: 8
Ingredients:
4 cups of cauliflower florets
2 tablespoons of extra virgin olive oil
¼ teaspoon of salt
¼ teaspoon of smoked paprika
¼ teaspoon of garlic powder
½ cup of sugar free hot sauce I used Archie Moore's brand
Dairy Free Ranch Dressing
1 cup organic mayonnaise
½ cup of Silk unsweetened coconut milk
1 teaspoon of garlic powder
1 teaspoon of onion powder
¼ teaspoon of pepper
1 tablespoon of fresh lemon juice
¼ cup fresh chopped parsley
Get Ingredients Powered by Chicory
Directions:
First heat oven to 400 degrees F. Spray baking sheet with nonstick olive oil cooking spray. Place florets in a large bowl and toss with olive oil. In a small bowl mix the salt, paprika and garlic powder together with hot sauce. Add the hot sauce into cauliflower bowl and stir well until well coated. Spread cauliflower out evenly on baking sheet and bake for 30 minutes. Whisk ingredients together and pour into a mason jar. Cover and refrigerate until ready to serve with cauli bites.
Nutrition:
Calories: 123, Fat: 16g, Carbohydrates: 12g, Fiber: 3g, Protein: 39g

Philly Cheesesteak Stuffed Mushrooms

Preparation Time: 15 minutes

Cooking Time: 15 minutes

Ingredients:

24 oz. baby bella mushrooms

1 cup chopped red pepper

1 cup chopped onion

2 tablespoons butter

1 teaspoon salt divided

½ teaspoon of pepper divided

1 pound of beef sirloin shaved or thinly sliced against the grain

4 ounces of provolone cheese

Get Ingredients Powered by Chicory

Directions:

First heat oven to 350 degrees. Remove stems from mushrooms and place mushrooms on a greased baby sheet. Sprinkle with ½ teaspoon of salt and ¼ teaspoon of pepper on both sides and bake for 15 minutes. Set aside. Melt 1 tablespoon butter in a large skillet and cook pepper and onions until soft. Then season with ½ teaspoon of salt and ¼ teaspoon of pepper. Remove from the skillet and set aside. In the same skillet, melt the remaining tablespoon of butter and cook the meat to your preference. Add the provolone cheese and stir until completely melted. Return back the veggies. Add mixture into the mushrooms, top with more cheese if you like and bake for 5 minutes. Serve and enjoy.

Nutrition:

Calories: 435, Fat: 16g, Carbohydrates: 27g, Fiber: 3g, Protein: 39g

Greek Cookies

Preparation Time: 20 minutes
Cooking Time: 725 minutes
Servings:6
Ingredients:
½ cup Plain yogurt
½ teaspoon baking powder
2 tablespoons Erythritol
1 teaspoon almond extract
½ teaspoon ground clove
½ teaspoon orange zest, grated
3 tablespoons walnuts, chopped
1 cup wheat flour
1 teaspoon butter, softened
1 tablespoon honey
3 tablespoons water
Directions:
In the mixing bowl mix up together Plain yogurt, baking powder, Erythritol, almond extract, ground cloves orange zest, flour, and butter.

Knead the non-sticky dough. Add olive oil if the dough is very sticky and knead it well.

Then make the log from the dough and cut it into small pieces.

Roll every piece of dough into the balls and transfer in the lined with baking paper tray.

Press the balls gently and bake for 25 minutes at 350F.

Meanwhile, heat up together honey and water. Simmer the liquid for 1 minute and remove from the heat.

When the cookies are cooked, remove them from the oven and let them cool for 5 minutes.

Then pour the cookies with sweet honey water and sprinkle with walnuts.

Cool the cookies.

Nutrition
calories 134, fat 3.4, fiber 0.9, carbs 26.1, protein 4.3

Ham And Dill Pickle Bites

Preparation Time: 5 minutes

Cooking Time: 45 minutes

Ingredients:

Dill pickles

Thin deli ham slices

Cream cheese (or use whipped cream cheese if you prefer)

Directions:

Let the cream cheese sit for at least 30 minutes at room temperature before you make these. Cut dill pickles lengthwise into sixths, depending on how thick the pickles are. You need as many cut pickles spears as you have ham slices. Spread each slice of ham with a very thin layer of cream cheese. Place a dill pickle on the edge of each ham slice. Then roll up the ham around the dill pickle, and place toothpicks where you want each piece to be cut. Arrange on plate and serve. Enjoy.

Nutrition:

Calories: 217, Fat: 11g, Carbohydrates: 17g, Fiber: 6g, Protein: 20g

Easy Flavored Potatoes Mix

Preparation Time: 10 minutes
Cooking Time: 25 minutes
Servings: 2
Ingredients:
4 potatoes, thinly sliced
2 tablespoons olive oil
1 fennel bulb, thinly sliced
1 tablespoon dill, chopped
8 cherry tomatoes, halved
Salt and black pepper to the taste
Directions:
Preheat your air fryer to 365 degrees F and add the oil.

Add potato slices, fennel, dill, tomatoes, salt and pepper, toss, cover and cook for 25 minutes.

Divide potato mix between plates and serve.

Enjoy!
Nutrition:
calories 240, fat 3, fiber 2, carbs 5, protein 12

Eggplant Sandwich

Preparation Time: 30 minutes
Cooking Time: 30 minutes
Servings: 2
Ingredients:

1 eggplant, sliced

2 teaspoons parsley, dried

Salt and black pepper to the taste

½ cup vegan breadcrumbs

½ teaspoon Italian seasoning

½ teaspoon garlic powder

½ teaspoon onion powder

2 tablespoons almond milk

4 vegan bread slices

Cooking spray

½ cup avocado mayo

¾ cup tomato sauce

A handful basil, chopped

Directions:

Season eggplant slices with salt and pepper, leave aside for 30 minutes and then pat dry them well.

In a bowl, mix parsley with breadcrumbs, Italian seasoning, onion and garlic powder, salt and black pepper and stir.

In another bowl, mix milk with vegan mayo and also stir well.

Brush eggplant slices with mayo mix, dip them in breadcrumbs mix, place them on a lined baking sheet, spray with cooking oil, introduce baking sheet in your air fryer's basket and cook them at 400 degrees F for 15 minutes, flipping them halfway.

Brush each bread slice with olive oil and arrange 2 of them on a working surface.

Add baked eggplant slices, spread tomato sauce and basil and top with the other bread slices, greased side down.

Divide between plates and serve.

Enjoy!

Nutrition:

calories 324, fat 16, fiber 4, carbs 19, protein 12

No Bake Oat Cookies

Preparation Time: 30 minutes
Cooking Time: 0 minutes
Servings: 24
Ingredients:

½ cup plain soymilk

1¾ cups sugar

½ cup Vegan butter

1 teaspoon vanilla extract

3½ cups quick cooking oats

¼ cup unsweetened cocoa powder

½ cup smooth or crunchy peanut butter

Directions:

In a small pot combine the milk, butter, sugar, peanut butter and vanilla and cook until smooth and creamy

In a large bowl combine the oats and cocoa powder.

Pour the warm milk mixture over the oats and stir until all the ingredients have combined.

Place dollops of mixture onto a waxed paper lined cookie sheet and let cool for about half an hour.

Nutrition:

Calories 171, Fat 6.7g, Carbs 25.5g, Dietary Fiber 2.0g, Protein 3.3g

Chocolate Coconut Quinoa Slices

Preparation Time: 10 minutes
Cooking Time: 50 minutes
Servings: 12
Ingredients:

¾ cup quinoa

½ cup dried chopped dates

3 tablespoons maple syrup

2 tablespoons olive oil

2 tablespoons ground flaxseed

½ teaspoon almond extract

¼ teaspoon salt

½ cup chocolate protein powder

½ cup whole wheat flour

¼ cup Vegan chocolate chips

¼ cup shredded coconut

Water

Directions:

Pre-heat the oven to 350°F.

Prepare an 8 x 8 ovenproof baking dish. Grease lightly with oil.

Rinse the quinoa in cold water and leave to soak for about 10 minutes.

Drain the quinoa. Place 1 cup of water in a small saucepan bring to the boil. Add the quinoa and simmer over a low heat for about 12 minutes. Cool.

In a food processor combine the cooked quinoa, dates, maple syrup, olive oil, flaxseed, almond extract and salt.

Process until fairly smooth.

In a separate bowl stir together the chocolate protein powder, flour chocolate chips and coconut.

Fold the dry mixture into the wet mixture with a flat spatula or knife.

Press into the prepared baking dish. Even out the top.

Bake for about 25 minutes, until firm.

Cool and then slice into bars.

Store in an airtight container for about a week or freeze up to 3 months.

Nutrition:

Calories 160, Fat 4.7g, Carbs 22.4g, Dietary Fiber 2.9g, Protein 9.0g

Apple And Nut Chews

Preparation Time: 15 minutes
Cooking Time: 40 minutes
Servings: 24
Ingredients:

½ cup whole wheat flour

¾ cup oats

1 cup grape nuts cereal

¾ cup golden raisins

1 cup shredded coconut (sweetened or unsweetened)

¼ cup raw almonds

½ cup raw cashews

2 teaspoons ground cinnamon

2 tablespoons ground flax seeds

¼ cup warm water

15 ounce can Great Northern Beans

1 cup chopped fresh dates

1 teaspoon vanilla extract

2 tablespoons maple syrup or brown sugar

1 tablespoon vegetable oil

½ cup apple sauce

Directions:

Preheat your oven to 350° F.

Grease a 9 x 13 oven dish

Wash and drain the beans to remove any salt. Chop roughly.

Mix the flaxseed with the warm water and set aside to thicken.

Combine the flour, oats, grape not cereal, raisins, coconut, nuts and cinnamon in a large bowl.

Mix the beans, flaxseed mix, dates, vanilla, maple syrup, oil and apple sauce together and add to the dry ingredients.

Mix well.

Press into the prepared oven dish.

Bake for about 25 minutes, rotating the dish after 15 minutes.

Remove from the oven and cool.

Cut into 24 small bars.

Either leave unwrapped for hard chewier bars or wrap for a softer texture.

These will keep for about a week unfrozen. Freeze them if you want to keep them for longer.

Nutrition:

Calories 138, Fat 4.1g, Carbs 23.8g, Dietary Fiber 3.4g, Protein 3.7g

Banana Carob Bars With A Chili Twist

Preparation Time: 10 minutes
Cooking Time: 0 minutes
Servings: 8
Ingredients:

¼ cup Medjool dates

½ jalapeno pepper

1 small ripe banana

½ cup cooked buckwheat

¼ cup roasted carob powder

¼ cup white chia seeds

¼ cup roasted macadamia nuts

Pinch of sea salt

Raw sesame seeds to sprinkle

Directions:

Place all of the ingredients into a food processor.

Process by pulsing until all of the ingredients are well mixed and have come together.

Press into 8 small bars or round cakes if you prefer.

Sprinkle with sesame seeds.

Nutrition:

Calories 90, Fat 4.4g, Carbs 13.4g, Dietary Fiber 3.3g, Protein 2.0g

Lemon Mousse

Preparation Time: 10 minutes + chill time

Cooking Time: 10 minutes

Serving: 4

Ingredients:

1 cup coconut cream

8 ounces cream cheese, soft

¼ cup fresh lemon juice

3 pinches salt

1 teaspoon lemon liquid stevia

Directions:

Preheat your oven to 350 °F

Grease a ramekin with butter

Beat cream, cream cheese, fresh lemon juice, salt and lemon liquid stevia in a mixer

Pour batter into ramekin

Bake for 10 minutes, then transfer the mousse to a serving glass

Let it chill for 2 hours and serve

Enjoy!

Nutrition:

Calories: 395

Fat: 31g

Carbohydrates: 3g

Protein: 5g

Jalapeno Crisp

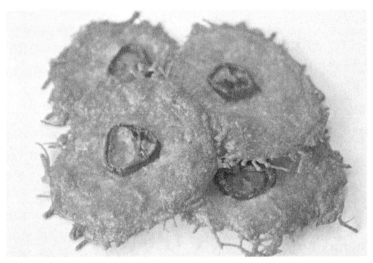

Preparation Time: 10 minutes

Cooking Time: 1 hour 15 minutes

Serving: 20

Ingredients:

1 cup sesame seeds

1 cup sunflower seeds

1 cup flaxseeds

½ cup hulled hemp seeds

3 tablespoons Psyllium husk

1 teaspoon salt

1 teaspoon baking powder

2 cups of water

Directions:

Pre-heat your oven to 350 °F

Take your blender and add seeds, baking powder, salt, and Psyllium husk

Blend well until a sand-like texture appears

Stir in water and mix until a batter forms

Allow the batter to rest for 10 minutes until a dough-like thick mixture forms

Pour the dough onto a cookie sheet lined with parchment paper

Spread it evenly, making sure that it has a thickness of ¼ inch thick all around

Bake for 75 minutes in your oven

Remove and cut into 20 spices

Allow them to cool for 30 minutes and enjoy!

Nutrition:

Calories: 156

Fat: 13g

Carbohydrates: 2g

Protein: 5g

Raspberry Popsicle

Preparation Time: 2 hours
Cooking Time: 15 minutes
Serving: 4
Ingredients:
1 ½ cups raspberries
2 cups of water
Directions:
Take a pan and fill it up with water
Add raspberries
Place it over medium heat and bring to water to a boil
Reduce the heat and simmer for 15 minutes
Remove heat and pour the mix into Popsicle molds
Add a popsicle stick and let it chill for 2 hours
Serve and enjoy!
Nutrition:
Calories: 58
Fat: 0.4g
Carbohydrates: 0g
Protein: 1.4g

Easy Fudge

Preparation Time: 15 minutes + chill time
Cooking Time: 5 minutes
Serving: 25
Ingredients:

1 ¾ cups of coconut butter

1 cup pumpkin puree

1 teaspoon ground cinnamon

¼ teaspoon ground nutmeg

1 tablespoon coconut oil

Directions:

Take an 8x8 inch square baking pan and line it with aluminum foil

Take a spoon and scoop out the coconut butter into a heated pan and allow the butter to melt

Keep stirring well and remove from the heat once fully melted

Add spices and pumpkin and keep straining until you have a grain-like texture

Add coconut oil and keep stirring to incorporate everything

Scoop the mixture into your baking pan and evenly distribute it

Place wax paper on top of the mixture and press gently to straighten the top

Remove the paper and discard

Allow it to chill for 1-2 hours

Once chilled, take it out and slice it up into pieces

Enjoy!

Nutrition:

Calories: 120

Fat: 10g

Carbohydrates: 5g

Protein: 1.2g

Blueberry Muffins

Preparation Time: 10 minutes
Cooking Time: 30 minutes
Serving: 4
Ingredients:
1 cup almond flour
Pinch of salt
1/8 teaspoon baking soda
1 whole egg
2 tablespoons coconut oil, melted
½ cup of coconut milk
¼ cup fresh blueberries
Directions:
Preheat your oven to 350 °F
Line a muffin tin with paper muffin cups
Add almond flour, salt, baking soda to a bowl and mix, keep it on the side
Take another bowl and add egg, coconut oil, coconut milk, and mix
Add mix to flour mix and gently combine until incorporated
Mix in blueberries and fill the cupcakes tins with batter
Bake for 20-25 minutes
Enjoy!
Nutrition:
Calories: 167
Fat: 15g
Carbohydrates: 2.1g
Protein: 5.2g

The Coconut Loaf

Preparation Time: 15 minutes
Cooking Time: 40 minutes
Serving: 4
Ingredients:
1 ½ tablespoons coconut flour
¼ teaspoon baking powder
1/8 teaspoon salt
1 tablespoon coconut oil, melted
1 whole egg
Directions:
Preheat your oven to 350 °F
Add coconut flour, baking powder, salt
Add coconut oil, eggs and stir well until mixed
Leave the batter for several minutes
Pour half the batter onto the baking pan
Spread it to form a circle, repeat with remaining batter
Bake in the oven for 10 minutes
Once a golden brown texture comes, let it cool and serve
Enjoy!
Nutrition:
Calories: 297
Fat: 14g
Carbohydrates: 15g
Protein: 15g

Chocolate Parfait

Preparation Time: 2 hours
Cooking Time: 0 minutes
Serving: 4
Ingredients:
2 tablespoons cocoa powder
1 cup almond milk
1 tablespoon chia seeds
Pinch of salt
½ teaspoon vanilla extract
Directions:
Take a bowl and add cocoa powder, almond milk, chia seeds, vanilla extract, and stir
Transfer to dessert glass and place in your fridge for 2 hours
Serve and enjoy!
Nutrition:
Calories: 130
Fat: 5g
Carbohydrates: 7g
Protein: 16g

Cauliflower Bagel

Preparation Time: 10 minutes
Cooking Time: 30 minutes
Serving: 12
Ingredients:
1 large cauliflower, divided into florets and roughly chopped
¼ cup nutritional yeast
¼ cup almond flour
½ teaspoon garlic powder
1 ½ teaspoon fine sea salt
2 whole eggs
1 tablespoon sesame seeds
Directions:
Preheat your oven to 400 °F
Line a baking sheet with parchment paper, keep it on the side
Blend cauliflower in a food processor and transfer to a bowl
Add nutritional yeast, almond flour, garlic powder and salt to a bowl, mix
Take another bowl and whisk in eggs, add to cauliflower mix
Give the dough a stir
Incorporate the mix into the egg mix
Make balls from the dough, making a hole using your thumb into each ball
Arrange them on your prepped sheet, flattening them into bagel shapes
Sprinkle sesame seeds and bake for half an hour
Remove the oven and let them cool, enjoy!
Nutrition:
Calories: 152
Fat: 10g
Carbohydrates: 4g
Protein: 4g

Almond Crackers

Preparation Time: 10 minutes
Cooking Time: 20 minutes
Serving: 40 crackers
Ingredients:
1 cup almond flour
¼ teaspoon baking soda
¼ teaspoon salt
1/8 teaspoon black pepper
3 tablespoons sesame seeds
1 egg, beaten
Salt and pepper to taste
Directions:
Preheat your oven to 350 °F
Line two baking sheets with parchment paper and keep them on the side
Mix the dry ingredients into a large bowl and add egg, mix well and form a dough
Divide dough into two balls
Roll out the dough between two pieces of parchment paper
Cut into crackers and transfer them to prep a baking sheet
Bake for 15-20 minutes
Repeat until all the dough has been used up
Leave crackers to cool and serve
Enjoy!
Nutrition:
Calories: 302
Fat: 28g
Carbohydrates: 4g
Protein: 9g

Cashew And Almond Butter

Preparation Time: 5 minutes
Cooking Time: 0 minutes
Serving: 1 ½ cups
Ingredients:
1 cup almonds, blanched
1/3 cup cashew nuts
2 tablespoons coconut oil
Salt as needed
½ teaspoon cinnamon
Directions:
Preheat your oven to 350 °F
Bake almonds and cashews for 12 minutes
Let them cool
Transfer to a food processor and add remaining ingredients
Add oil and keep blending until smooth
Serve and enjoy!
Nutrition:
Calories: 205
Fat: 19g
Carbohydrates: g
Protein: 2.8g

Basic Meat Loaf

Preparation Time: 5 minutes
Cooking Time: 45 minutes
Servings: 8
Ingredients:
1 lb. lean ground turkey
1 egg white
1 tablespoon lemon juice
½ cup plain breadcrumbs
½ teaspoon onion powder
½ teaspoon Italian seasoning
¼ teaspoon black pepper
½ cup chopped onions
½ cup diced green bell pepper
¼ cup of water
Directions:
Mix the meat with the lemon juice thoroughly in a bowl.
Stir in the remaining seasoning, breadcrumbs, egg white, veggies, and water.
Mix well, then spread this mixture in a loaf pan.
Bake the crumbly meatloaf for 45 minutes at 350 degrees F.
Slice and serve.
Nutrition:
Calories 118
Total Fat 4.6g
Saturated Fat 1.4g
Cholesterol 41mg
Sodium 98mg
Carbohydrate 6.5g
Dietary Fiber 0.5g
Sugars 1.3g
Protein 12.8g
Calcium 24mg
Phosphorous 241mg
Potassium 223mg

Cereal Munch

Preparation Time: 5 minutes
Cooking Time: 45 minutes
Servings: 3
Ingredients:
3 cups cereal, salt-free
1 ½ cups oyster crackers, salt-free
2 ½ tablespoons butter, unsalted
½ cup pretzel twists, salt-free
½ tablespoon chili powder
1 pinch ground cumin
¼ teaspoon garlic powder
1 pinch cayenne pepper
¾ teaspoons lemon juice
Directions:
Brush a 10x15 inches pan with melted butter.
Toss the pretzels and crackers with the remaining ingredients in the baking tray.
Bake them for 45 minutes in the oven at 350 degrees F.
Toss the cereal munch every 15 minutes.
Serve.
Nutrition:
Calories 379
Total Fat 11.2g
Saturated Fat 1.8g
Cholesterol 0mg
Sodium 254mg
Carbohydrate 48.9g
Dietary Fiber 9.3g
Sugars 21.3g
Protein 8.3g
Calcium 28mg
Phosphorous 319mg
Potassium 365mg

Coconut Mandarin Salad

Preparation Time: 10 minutes
Cooking Time: 0 minutes
Servings: 6
Ingredients:

20 oz. can pineapple chunks

11 oz. canned mandarin oranges

10 oz. maraschino cherries, cut in halves

16 oz. sour cream

2 cups shredded sweetened coconut

Directions:

Toss the pineapples with the cherries, oranges, coconut, and sour cream in a bowl.

Serve fresh.

Nutrition:

Calories 372

Total Fat 24.9g

Saturated Fat 17.8g

Cholesterol 33mg

Sodium 49mg

Total Carbohydrate 36.2g

Dietary Fiber 4.3g

Sugars 28.8g

Protein 3.9g

Phosphorous 356mg

Potassium 464mg

Cream Dipped Cucumbers

Preparation Time: 10 minutes
Cooking Time: 0 minutes
Servings: 4
Ingredients:

1/2 cup sour cream

3 tablespoons white vinegar

1 teaspoon stevia

Pepper to taste

4 cucumbers, peeled and sliced

1 small sweet onion, cut in rings

Directions:

Use a medium-sized serving bowl.

Add in the cucumber, onion, and all the other ingredients.

Mix them well and refrigerate for 2 hours.

Toss again, serve and enjoy.

Nutrition:

Calories 127

Total Fat 6.4g

Saturated Fat 3.9g

Cholesterol 13mg

Sodium 23mg

Carbohydrate 9.2g

Dietary Fiber 1.9g

Sugars 4.2g

Protein 3.1g

Calcium 86mg

Phosphorous 172mg

Potassium 518mg

Barbecue Cups

Preparation Time: 5 minutes
Cooking Time: 20 minutes
Servings: 10
Ingredients:
¾ lb. lean ground turkey
½ cup spicy barbecue sauce
2 teaspoons onion flakes
1 dash garlic powder
1 (10-oz.) package low-fat biscuits
Directions:
Grease a suitable pan with cooking spray and place it over moderate heat.
Add the ground turkey and sauté it until golden brown.
Flatten the biscuits and place them in a muffin tray.
Press each biscuit in its muffin cup and divide the turkey in them.
Top the turkey with barbecue sauce, garlic powder, and onion flakes.
Bake for 12 minutes at 400 degrees F in a preheated oven.
Serve.
Nutrition:
Calories 143
Total Fat 6.3g
Saturated Fat 1.8g
Cholesterol 25mg
Sodium 329mg
Carbohydrate 13.1g
Dietary Fiber 0.2g
Sugars 2.7g
Protein 8.6g
Calcium 21mg
Phosphorous 367mg
Potassium 164mg

Spiced Pretzels

Preparation Time: 5 minutes
Cooking Time: 1 hour 15 minutes
Servings: 10
Ingredients:
1 teaspoon ground cayenne pepper
1 teaspoon lemon pepper
1 1/2 teaspoons garlic powder
1 oz. dry Ranch-style dressing
3/4 cup vegetable oil
15 oz. packages mini pretzels
Directions:
Switch the oven to 175 degrees F to preheat.
Spread the pretzels on a cooking sheet and break them into pieces.
Whisk the oil with the garlic powder, lemon pepper, ground cayenne pepper, and ranch dressing in a bowl.
Pour this oil dressing over the pretzels and toss well to coat.
Bake the pretzels for approximately 1 hour then flip them to bake for another 15 minutes.
Serve fresh and warm.
Nutrition:
Calories 311
Total Fat 18.6g
Saturated Fat 3.2g
Cholesterol 0mg
Sodium 270mg
Carbohydrate 33.2g
Dietary Fiber 1.6g
Sugars 0g
Protein 3g
Calcium 1mg
Phosphorous 371mg
Potassium 6mg

Cauliflower With Mustard Sauce

Preparation Time: 5 minutes
Cooking Time: 10 minutes
Servings: 4
Ingredients:

1 head cauliflower, separated into florets

1/2 cup mayonnaise

1/4 cup Dijon mustard

1 cup sharp Cheddar cheese, shredded

Directions:

Whisk the mayonnaise with the mustard and cheese in a bowl.

Add the cauliflower florets in boiling water in a pot and cook until they are tender.

Drain the cauliflower then toss its florets with the mayo mixture.

Spread the cauliflower mixture in a baking pan.

Broil it for 5 minutes until the cheese is melted.

Serve fresh.

Nutrition:

Calories 255

Total Fat 19.9g

Saturated Fat 7.5g

Cholesterol 37mg

Sodium 582mg

Carbohydrate 11.7g

Dietary Fiber 2.2g

Sugars 3.8g

Protein 9.3g

Calcium 231mg

Phosphorous 97mg

Potassium 253mg

Pineapple Cabbage Coleslaw

Preparation Time: 10 minutes

Cooking Time: 0 minutes

Servings: 12

Ingredients:

12 oz. (bag) broccoli coleslaw

12 oz. Napa cabbage, finely shredded

20 oz. (can) unsweetened pineapple, drained

1/2 cup green onions, sliced

1 cup mayonnaise

1 tablespoon seasoned rice vinegar

1 teaspoon coarse ground black pepper

Directions:

Toss the cabbage with the broccoli, and all the other ingredients in a salad bowl.

Refrigerate this coleslaw for at least 1 hour.

Serve.

Nutrition:

Calories 186

Total Fat 12.7g

Saturated Fat 2g

Cholesterol 5mg

Sodium 224mg

Carbohydrate 18g

Dietary Fiber 2.1g

Sugars 10.4g

Protein 2g

Calcium 42mg

Phosphorous 106mg

Potassium 139mg

Seafood Croquettes

Preparation Time: 5 minutes
Cooking Time: 20 minutes
Servings: 8
Ingredients:
14.75 oz. packed salmon
2 egg whites
¼ cup chopped onion
½ teaspoon black pepper
½ cup plain breadcrumbs
2 tablespoons lemon juice
½ teaspoon ground mustard
¼ cup regular mayonnaise
Directions:
Drain the packed salmon and transfer it to a bowl.
Stir in all the other ingredients except the oil and mix well.
Make 8 patties out of this mixture and keep them aside.
Add the oil to a pan and place it over medium-high heat.
Add 4 patties at a time and sear them for 3 minutes per side.
Cook the remaining four in the same manner until golden brown.
Serve.
Nutrition:
Calories 282
Total Fat 12g
Saturated Fat 2.6g
Cholesterol 66mg
Sodium 202mg
Carbohydrate 7.4g
Dietary Fiber 0.4g
Sugars 1.3g
Protein 12.6g
Calcium 88mg
Phosphorous 137mg
Potassium 253mg

Sweet Rice Salad

Preparation Time: 10 minutes
Cooking Time: 0 minutes
Servings: 6
Ingredients:
3 tablespoons apricot jam
1 tablespoon water
1 tablespoon lemon juice
7 tablespoons mayonnaise
6 oz. long-grain rice, cooked & rinsed
1 oz. onion, finely chopped
2 apples, chopped
8 cherry tomatoes
Directions:
Mix the rice with the apples, tomatoes, and onion in a salad bowl.
Whisk the apricot jam and the rest of the dressing ingredients in a small bowl.
Pour this dressing into the rice salad and mix well.
Serve.
Nutrition:
Calories 265
Total Fat 6.4g
Saturated Fat 1g
Cholesterol 4mg
Sodium 137mg
Carbohydrate 49.2g
Dietary Fiber 4.3g
Sugars 17.8g
Protein 4g
Calcium 30mg
Phosphorous 258mg
Potassium 520mg

Herbed Shrimp Spread

Preparation Time: 10 minutes
Cooking Time: 0 minutes
Servings: 8
Ingredients:
1/2 lb. shrimp, cooked, peeled and deveined
1/2 cup reduced-fat sour cream
1/2 cup light mayonnaise
2 scallions, coarsely chopped
1 teaspoon lemon zest, finely grated
2 teaspoons fresh lemon juice
1/4 cup parsley, chopped
Directions:
Begin by tossing the minced shrimp with the sour cream in a bowl.
Add in the mayonnaise, scallions, lemon juice and lemon zest.
Mix well and garnish with parsley.
Serve the spread.
Nutrition:
Calories 118
Total Fat 8.3g
Saturated Fat 2.7g
Cholesterol 65mg
Sodium 177mg
Carbohydrate 4.6g
Dietary Fiber 0.2g
Sugars 1.1g
Protein 6.7g
Calcium 35mg
Phosphorous 203mg
Potassium 95mg

Almond Caramel Corn

Preparation Time: 10 minutes
Cooking Time: 1 hour 5 minutes
Servings: 30
Ingredients:
12 cups popped popcorn
3 cups unblanched whole almonds
1 cup brown Swerve
½ cup butter
¼ cup light corn syrup
½ teaspoon baking soda
Directions:
Take a suitable roasting pan and spread the almonds and popcorn in it.
Whisk the Swerve with the butter and corn syrup in a heavy saucepan.
Stir-fry this corn syrup for about 5 minutes up to a boil then add in the baking soda.
Pour this corn sauce over the popcorn and almonds in the pan.
Bake the popcorn mixture for approximately 1 hour at 200 degrees F in the oven.
Stir well then serve.
Nutrition:
Calories 120
Total Fat 8g
Saturated Fat 2.3g
Cholesterol 8mg
Sodium 45mg
Carbohydrate 6.5g
Dietary Fiber 1.7g
Sugars 1.1g
Protein 2.5g
Calcium 31mg
Phosphorous 23mg
Potassium 88mg

Jalapeno Tomato Salsa

Preparation Time: 10 minutes
Cooking Time: 0 minutes
Servings: 4
Ingredients:

4 jalapeños, seeded and chopped

3 garlic cloves, peeled

1/2 white onion, chopped

2 lb. tomatoes, quartered

Juice of 1/2 lime

Directions:

Add the jalapeños, garlic, onion, tomatoes, and lime juice into a blender.

Blend this salsa mixture until it gets chunky.

Serve fresh.

Nutrition:

Calories 32

Total Fat 0.3g

Saturated Fat 0g

Cholesterol 0mg

Sodium 638mg

Carbohydrate 5.3g

Dietary Fiber 1.6g

Sugars 3.2g

Protein 1.1g

Calcium 13mg

Phosphorous 33mg

Potassium 244mg

Blue Cheese Pear Salad

Preparation Time: 10 minutes
Cooking Time: 0 minutes
Servings: 6
Ingredients:
1/2 cup sliced red onion
1 Bosc pear, cored and sliced
1/2 cup chopped candied pecans
1/2 cup crumbled blue cheese
1/4 cup maple syrup
1/3 cup apple cider vinegar
1/2 cup mayonnaise
2 tablespoons brown Swerve
1/4 teaspoon black pepper
1/4 cup olive oil
Directions:
Add all the pear salad ingredients to a salad bowl.
Toss them well and refrigerate for 1 hour.
Serve.
Nutrition:
Calories 229
Total Fat 13.8g
Saturated Fat 3.3g
Cholesterol 14mg
Sodium 300mg
Carbohydrate 20g
Dietary Fiber 1.8g
Sugars 13g
Protein 4.2g
Calcium 84mg
Phosphorous 54mg
Potassium 159mg

Sweet Popped Popcorn

Preparation Time: 5 minutes
Cooking Time: 5 minutes
Servings: 4
Ingredients:

2 ¾ oz. popped popcorn

2 tablespoons butter

2 tablespoons corn syrup

2 tablespoons brown Swerve

1 teaspoon oil

Directions:

Whisk the corn syrup, brown Swerve and oil in a saucepan.

Stir-fry the corn syrup mixture for 5 minutes then remove it from heat.

Add the butter and mix well, then let the mixture cool.

Toss in the popped popcorn.

Serve.

Nutrition:

Calories 224

Total Fat 7.1g

Saturated Fat 3.9g

Cholesterol 15mg

Sodium 178mg

Carbohydrate 21g

Dietary Fiber 0.2g

Sugars 8.7g

Protein 1.2g

Calcium 8mg

Phosphorous 11mg

Potassium 38mg

Lunch Recipes

Baked Cauliflower And Broccoli Mac And Cheese

Preparation Time: 10 minutes

Cooking Time: 40 minutes

Servings – 8

Ingredients

12 ounces penne pasta, cooked

3 tablespoons all-purpose white flour

2 cups broccoli florets, steamed

½ cup white onion, chopped

2 cups cauliflower florets, steamed

¼ teaspoon minced garlic

2 tablespoons brown mustard

4 tablespoons unsalted butter

½ teaspoon ground black pepper

¼ teaspoon nutmeg

1 cup panko bread crumbs

1 cup Swiss cheese, shredded

½ cup parmesan cheese, shredded

1 cup white cheddar cheese, shredded

2 ½ cups rice drink

Directions:

Switch on the oven, then set it to 350°F and let it preheat.

Take a medium-sized pot, place it over medium heat, add 3 tablespoons butter and when it melts, add onion and garlic and cook for 4 minutes until tender.

Stir in flour, cook for 1 minute until thickened, and then stir in mustard.

Mix all the three cheeses, add 2/3 of the cheeses mixture, stir well until it has melted, remove the pot from heat, add pasta, broccoli and cauliflower florets and stir until well coated.

Take a 9-by-12 baking pan, grease it well, spoon in prepared pasta mixture, top with remaining cheese mixture, and then bake for 30 minutes.

Then melt the remaining butter, add bread crumbs, stir until mixed, cook for 2 minutes until golden, then top it over pasta mixture after 30 minutes and continue baking for 10 minutes until the top has turned brown.

Serve straight away.

Nutrition:

Calories – 442

Fat – 18 g

Protein – 18 g

Carbohydrates – 52 g

Fiber – 2.2 g

Caraway Cabbage And Rice

Preparation Time: 5 minutes
Cooking Time: 10 minutes

Servings – 2

Ingredients

1 cup of rice, cooked

¼ cup mandarin oranges

1 tablespoon white onion, chopped

1 cup cabbage, shredded

½ teaspoon caraway seed

1 tablespoon Worcestershire sauce

¼ cup water

Directions:

Take a frying pan, grease it with oil, place it over medium heat, add onion and cabbage and cook for 5 minutes until cabbage leaves wilted.

Stir in caraway seeds, Worcestershire sauce, and water, continue cooking for 3 minutes, add oranges and stir until rice until well combined.

Serve straight away.

Nutrition:

Calories – 142

Fat – 0 g

Protein – 3 g

Carbohydrates – 31 g

Fiber – 2.4 g

Gratin Pasta With Watercress And Chicken

Preparation Time: 10 minutes
Cooking Time: 50 minutes
Servings – 4
Ingredients
2 cups pasta shells, cooked
1 cup chicken, shredded and cooked
1 small white onion, peeled and chopped
1 cup fresh watercress
1 teaspoon minced garlic
¼ teaspoon ground black pepper
1 tablespoon olive oil
½ cup Parmesan cheese, grated
1 2/3 cup béchamel sauce

Directions:

Take a medium-sized skillet pan, place it over medium heat, add oil and when hot, add onion and garlic, and cook for 4 minutes until sauted.

Then stir in chicken and watercress until mixed and continue cooking for 3 minutes until leaves of watercress have wilted.

Add pasta, pour in half of the béchamel sauce, mix until coated, and spoon the mixture into a greased baking dish.

Cover pasta with remaining béchamel sauce, sprinkle cheese on top and bake for 40 minutes until cheese has melts and pasta is bubbling.

Serve straight away.

Nutrition:

Calories – 345

Fat – 13 g

Protein – 19 g

Carbohydrates – 38 g

Fiber – 2.1 g

Orzo And Vegetables

Preparation Time: 5 minutes
Cooking Time: 20 minutes
Servings – 6
Ingredients
1 medium carrot, peeled and shredded
1 small white onion, peeled and chopped
1 small zucchini, chopped
½ cup frozen green peas
½ teaspoon minced garlic
¼ teaspoon salt
¼ teaspoon ground black pepper
1 teaspoon curry powder
2 tablespoons olive oil
¼ cup Parmesan cheese, grated
3 cups chicken broth, low-sodium
2 tablespoons parsley, chopped
1 cup orzo pasta, uncooked

Directions:
Take a large skillet pan, place it over medium heat, add oil and when hot, add onion, garlic, carrot, and zucchini and cook for 5 minutes until sauted.

Stir in salt and curry powder, pour in the broth, stir until mixed and bring the mixture to a bowl.

Then stir in pasta, bring it to a boil, switch heat to medium-low level, and simmer for 10 minutes all the liquid has absorbed by the pasta.

Stir in remaining ingredients until mixed and cook for 3 minutes, or until hot.

Serve straight away.

Nutrition:
Calories – 176
Fat – 4 g
Protein – 10 g
Carbohydrates – 25 g
Fiber – 2.6 g

Lemon Rice With Vegetables

Preparation Time: 5 minutes
Cooking Time: 35 minutes
Servings – 5
Ingredients
10 tablespoons white rice, uncooked
1 ½ cups mushrooms, sliced
½ cup celery, sliced
¼ cup white onion, chopped
1/8 teaspoon ground black pepper
1/8 teaspoon dried thyme
1/8 teaspoon herb seasoning
1 teaspoon grated lemon zest
3 tablespoons unsalted margarine
2 tablespoons lemon juice
1 ¼ cups water

Directions:
Take a large skillet pan, place it over medium heat, add 1 ½ tablespoons margarine and when it melts, add onion and celery and cook for 5 minutes.

Season vegetables with lemon zest, black pepper, thyme, and herb seasoning, stir in water and lemon juice, bring to a boil, stir in rice, bring the mixture, then switch heat to medium-low level and simmer for 20 minutes until rice is tender.

Meanwhile, take a small-sized skillet pan, place it over medium heat, add remaining margarine and when it melts, add mushrooms and cook for 5 minutes until tender.

When the rice has cooked, stir cooked mushrooms in it and serve immediately.

Nutrition:
Calories – 183
Fat – 7 g
Protein – 3 g
Carbohydrates – 27 g
Fiber – 0.7 g

Chicken And Asparagus Pasta

Preparation Time: 5 minutes
Cooking Time: 20 minutes
Servings – 8
Ingredients
8 ounces skinless chicken breasts, cubed
16 ounces penne pasta, cooked
1 pound asparagus spears, trimmed
½ teaspoon minced garlic
¼ teaspoon garlic powder
½ teaspoon ground black pepper
1 ½ teaspoons dried oregano
5 tablespoons olive oil
¼ cup feta cheese, crumbled
½ cup chicken broth, low-sodium

Directions:

Take a large skillet pan, place it over medium-high heat, add 3 tablespoons oil and when hot, add chicken cubes, stir in garlic powder and ¼ teaspoon black pepper and continue cooking for 5 minutes until cooked and browned.

When done, transfer chicken cubes to a plate lined with paper towels, then pour in chicken broth, add asparagus, season with oregano and remaining black pepper, and cook for 5 minutes until asparagus has steamed, covering the pan.

Then stir in chicken, cook for 3 minutes until warmed, stir in pasta, stir until mixed and cook for 5 minutes until hot, set aside until needed.

Drizzle with remaining oil, top with cheese, and serve.

Nutrition:

Calories – 376
Fat – 12 g
Protein – 18 g
Carbohydrates – 49 g
Fiber – 3 g

Hawaiian Rice

Preparation Time: 5 minutes
Cooking Time: 13 minutes
Servings – 6
Ingredients
½ cup pineapple tidbits, unsweetened
½ cup red bell pepper, chopped
½ cup mushrooms, chopped
1 teaspoon ginger root, minced
½ cup bean sprouts
½ tablespoon soy sauce, reduced-sodium
¼ teaspoon salt
2 cups brown rice, cooked

Directions:

Take a frying pan, spray it with oil, place it over medium heat and when hot, add all the vegetables and cook for 5 minutes until sauted.

Then stir in ginger and pineapple, drizzle with soy sauce, season with salt and cook for 3 minutes, or until hot.

Stir in rice until well mixed, cook for 3 minutes until hot, and then serve.

Nutrition:

Calories – 97
Fat – 1 g
Protein – 2 g
Carbohydrates – 20 g
Fiber – 1.8 g

Mexican Rice

Preparation Time: 10 minutes
Cooking Time: 30 minutes
Servings – 6
Ingredients
¼ cup white onion, chopped
½ teaspoon minced garlic
¼ teaspoon salt
¼ cup canola oil
¼ cup tomato sauce, low-sodium
3 cups of water
1 cup white rice, uncooked

Directions:

Take a medium-sized skillet pan, place it over medium-high heat, add oil and when hot, add rice and cook for 5 minutes until browned.

Then add onion and garlic, stir until mixed, and cook for 3 minutes, or until tender.

Season with salt, pour in tomato sauce and water, stir until mixed, simmer for 20 minutes until rice has cooked, covering the pan.

Serve straight away.

Nutrition:

Calories – 194
Fat – 10 g
Protein – 2 g
Carbohydrates – 24 g
Fiber – 0.5 g

Shrimp Fried Rice

Preparation Time: 5 minutes
Cooking Time: 20 minutes

Servings – 4

Ingredients

4 cups white rice, cooked

½ cup small frozen shrimp, cooked

¾ cup white onion, chopped

1 cup frozen peas and carrots

3 tablespoons scallions, chopped

½ teaspoon minced garlic

1 tablespoon ginger root, grated

¼ teaspoon salt

¾ teaspoon ground black pepper

5 tablespoons peanut oil

4 eggs

Directions:

Take a large skillet pan, place it over medium-high heat, add
1 tablespoon peanut oil and when hot, add onion, season with
½ teaspoon black pepper, and cook for 2 minutes, or until
onions are tender.

Stir in scallions, ginger, and garlic, cook for 1 minute, add shrimps, stir until mixed, cook for 2 minutes until hot, then stir in carrots and peas and cook for 2 minutes until hot.

When done, transfer shrimps and vegetable mixture to a bowl, cover with a lid and set aside until required.

Return the skillet pan over medium heat, add 2 tablespoons oil, beat the eggs, pour it into the pan, cook for 3 minutes until eggs are scrambled to desired level and then transfer eggs to the bowl containing shrimps and vegetables.

Add remaining 1 tablespoon oil and when hot, add rice, stir until well coated, and cook for 2 minutes until hot.

Then season rice with salt and remaining black pepper, cook for 2 minutes, don't stir, then add eggs, shrimps, and vegetables, stir until mixed and cook for 3 minutes until hot.

Serve straight away.

Nutrition:

Calories – 421

Fat – 16 g

Protein – 16 g

Carbohydrates – 53 g

Fiber – 2.5 g

Vegetarian Egg Fried Rice

Preparation Time: 5 minutes
Cooking Time: 18 minutes
Servings – 6
Ingredients
4 cups white rice, cooked
1 cup diced tofu, extra-firm, drained
½ cup green onion, chopped
1 cup white onion, diced
1 cup fresh carrots, sliced
½ cup green peas
1 tablespoon ginger root, grated
1 teaspoon minced garlic
¼ teaspoon mustard powder
½ cup cilantro, chopped
3 tablespoons canola oil
1 tablespoon soy sauce, reduced-sodium
6 eggs, beaten

Directions:

Take a large skillet pan, place it over medium heat, add oil and when hot, add beaten eggs and cook the omelet for 3 minutes until eggs are cooked to the desired level.

Transfer omelet to a cutting board, let it cool for 5 minutes, and chop it, set aside until needed.

Add oil in the pan and when hot, add all the vegetables, stir in tofu, garlic, and ginger, season with mustard, cook for 5 minutes until carrots have softened.

Stir in rice and chopped eggs, drizzle with soy sauce, stir until well mixed and remove the pan from heat.

Garnish rice with green onion and cilantro and then serve.

Nutrition:

Calories – 343
Fat – 15 g
Protein – 15 g
Carbohydrates – 37 g
Fiber – 3.2 g

Autumn Orzo Salad

Preparation Time: 35 minutes
Cooking Time: 0 minutes

Servings – 4

Ingredients

1 medium apple, cored and diced

¾ cups orzo, cooked

¼ teaspoon ground black pepper

1 tablespoon fresh basil, chopped

2 tablespoons lemon juice

2 tablespoons olive oil

2 tablespoons almonds, sliced and blanched

Directions:

Take a medium-sized bowl, add all the ingredients in it (except for almonds), and stir until incorporated.

Take a baking dish, place prepared mixture in it, and place in the refrigerator for 30 minutes until chilled.

When ready to eat, garnish with almonds and serve.

Nutrition:

Calories – 227

Fat – 9 g

Protein – 5 g

Carbohydrates – 29 g

Fiber – 2.5 g

Blackened Shrimp And Pineapple Salad

Preparation Time: 10 minutes
Cooking Time: 8 minutes
Servings – 2
Ingredients
2 cups romaine lettuce, diced
½ of medium red bell pepper, sliced
1 ½ cups pineapple chunks
¼ cup corn kernels
14 large shrimp, peeled and deveined
1 tablespoon blackening seasoning, low-sodium
¼ teaspoon ground black pepper
1 tablespoon unsalted butter
1 tablespoon rice vinegar, unseasoned
1 tablespoon olive oil

Directions:

Prepare the shrimps by sprinkling them with blackening seasoning.

Take a skillet pan, place it over medium-high heat, add butter and when it melts, add prepared shrimps and cook for 3 minutes per side, or until curled.

Transfer shrimps to a plate lined with paper towels and set aside until cooled.

Prepare the salad by placing all the vegetables in a large salad bowl, add corn and pineapple, season with black pepper, drizzle with vinegar and oil and toss until well mixed.

Top the salad with the shrimps and serve.

Nutrition:

Calories – 260
Fat – 14 g
Protein – 13 g
Carbohydrates – 20 g
Fiber – 4.5 g

Green Pepper Slaw

Preparation Time: 5 minutes
Cooking Time: 0 minutes
Servings – 12
Ingredients
2 medium carrots, peeled and chopped
1 small head of cabbage, chopped
1 medium green bell pepper, cored and chopped
2 teaspoons celery seed
½ cup Splenda granulated sugar
½ cup apple cider vinegar
½ cup water

Directions:

Take a salad bowl, place carrot, cabbage, and bell pepper in it and mix well until combined.

Whisk together celery seeds, sugar, vinegar, and water until blended, drizzle it over the salad and toss until mixed.

Serve straight away.

Nutrition:

Calories – 76
Fat – 0 g
Protein – 1 g
Carbohydrates – 18 g
Fiber – 1 g

Italian Chicken Salad

Preparation Time: 1 hour and 10 minutes

Cooking Time: 0 minutes

Servings – 4

Ingredients

4 chicken breasts, cooked, ½-inch cubed

2 cups grilled summer squash, sliced

¼ cup sweet onion, chopped

1 medium orange bell pepper, cored and chopped

2 cups baby arugula

6 sprigs of parsley, leaves chopped

1/8 teaspoon cayenne pepper

¼ cup lemon juice

½ cup mayonnaise

Directions:

Prepare the dressing by placing mayonnaise in a bowl, add parsley, season with cayenne pepper, drizzle with lemon juice, and whisk until combined.

Place chicken cubes in a salad bowl, add remaining ingredients, except for arugula, stir until mixed, then drizzle with prepared dressing and toss until well coated.

Place the salad bowl in the refrigerator and chill for 1 hour and then serve the salad with arugula.

Nutrition:

Calories – 421

Fat – 29 g

Protein – 30 g

Carbohydrates – 10 g

Fiber – 2.2 g

Cranberries And Couscous Salad

Preparation Time: 10 minutes
Cooking Time: 0 minutes

Servings – 10

Ingredients

1 cup dried cranberries, sweetened

½ cup green onion, chopped

1 ½ cups couscous, cooked

½ cup celery, chopped

½ cup cucumber, chopped

2 teaspoons lemon zest

½ teaspoon ground cumin

1 tablespoon parsley, chopped

¼ teaspoon ground cayenne pepper

¼ cup lemon juice

1 tablespoon olive oil

Directions:

Take a large bowl, add couscous in it, drizzle with lemon juice, season with all the spices, and stir until combined.

Add remaining ingredients, stir until mixed, and then serve.

Nutrition:

Calories – 158

Fat – 2 g

Protein – 4 g

Carbohydrates – 31 g

Fiber – 2.5 g

Tuna Salad

Preparation Time: 10 minutes

Cooking Time: 0 minutes

Servings – 4

Ingredients

½ of large apple, cored and chopped

15 ounces tuna, packed in water, unsalted

½ of small white onion, peeled and chopped

1 celery stalk, chopped

1/8 teaspoon salt

1/8 teaspoon ground black pepper

3 tablespoons mayonnaise

Lettuce for serving

Directions:

Prepare the salad by taking a bowl, place tuna in it, add remaining ingredients in it (except for lettuce), and stir until mixed.

Place the salad on the lettuce and serve.

Nutrition:

Calories – 202

Fat – 9 g

Protein – 27 g

Carbohydrates – 3 g

Fiber – 0.8 g

Mixed Berry And Fruit Salad

Preparation Time: 1 hour and 5 minutes
Cooking Time: 0 minutes

Servings – 4

Ingredients

2 cups fresh strawberries, quartered

10 leaves of fresh basil

1 cup fresh blueberries

1 tablespoon Splenda granulated sugar

2 tablespoons white balsamic vinegar

¼ cup almond and coconut milk blend

Directions:

Take a large bowl, pour in the milk, and stir in sugar and vinegar until combined.

Add all the berries, toss well until combined, cover the bowl and place it into the refrigerator for 1 hour until chilled.

When ready to eat, stir basil into the salad and serve.

Nutrition:

Calories – 65

Fat – 1 g

Protein – 1 g

Carbohydrates – 13 g

Fiber – 2.4 g

Roasted Vegetable Salad

Preparation Time: 10 minutes
Cooking Time: 35 minutes
Servings – 8
Ingredients
6 cups baby leaf lettuce, chopped
1 small head cauliflower, cut into florets
5 medium carrots, peeled, 2-inch diced
½ cup pomegranate seeds
1 large turnip, peeled and diced
1 medium white onion, peeled and diced
¼ teaspoon ground black pepper
1 tablespoon Italian seasoning blend
¼ teaspoon yellow mustard
¼ teaspoon salt
1 ½ tablespoons maple syrup
3 tablespoons rice vinegar, unseasoned
6 tablespoons olive oil

Directions:

Switch on the oven, then set it to 425°F and let it preheat.

Meanwhile, take a large bowl, place all the vegetables in it, except for lettuce, season with Italian seasoning, drizzle with 3 tablespoons oil and toss until coated.

Take a baking sheet, place all the vegetables in it, and bake for 35 minutes until tender, turning halfway.

While vegetables are baking, prepare the dressing by placing remaining oil in a small bowl and whisk in salt, black pepper, mustard, vinegar, and maple syrup until combined.

When vegetables have roasted, transfer them to a salad bowl, add lettuce, drizzle with prepared dressing and toss until well coated.

Top the salad with pomegranate seeds and then serve.

Nutrition:

Calories – 160

Fat – 11 g

Protein – 2 g

Carbohydrates – 13 g

Fiber – 3.1 g

Chicken Pita Pizza

Preparation Time: 5 minutes
Cooking Time: 12 minutes

Servings – 2

Ingredients

4 ounces chicken, cooked and cubed

1/8 teaspoon garlic powder

¼ cup purple onion, chopped

3 tablespoons barbecue sauce, low-sodium

2 tablespoons feta cheese, crumbled

2 pita breads, about 6 ½ inches

Directions:

Switch on the oven, then set it to 350°F and let it preheat.

Take a baking sheet, spray it with oil, place pitas on it, spread 1 ½ tablespoon of sauce on each pita, then scatter with onions and chicken.

Sprinkle cheese and garlic powder on top of pitas and bake for 12 minutes until cooked.

Serve straight away.

Nutrition:

Calories – 320

Fat – 9 g

Protein – 23 g

Carbohydrates – 37 g

Fiber – 2.4 g

Cauliflower Steak Sandwiches

Preparation Time: 15 minutes
Cooking Time: 40 minutes
Servings – 4
Ingredients
1 medium head cauliflower
¼ cup chopped red onion
¼ teaspoon garlic powder
¼ teaspoon ground black pepper
¼ teaspoon onion powder
1/8 teaspoon salt
4 teaspoons mustard
3 tablespoons olive oil
4 lettuce leaves
2 tablespoons and 2 teaspoons mayonnaise
4 hamburger buns

Directions:

Switch on the oven, then set it to 400°F and then let it preheat. Prepare the cauliflower steaks by cutting four 1-inch thick slices and reserve the rest of cauliflower for future use.

Place oil in a small bowl, stir in salt, black pepper, onion powder, and garlic powder until mixed, and brush half of this mixture on both sides of cauliflower steaks.

Place the seasoned cauliflower steak on a baking sheet lined with parchment paper and bake for 40 minutes until cooked, flipping, and turning cauliflower halfway.

When done, sandwich a cauliflower steak into each bun, spread 2 teaspoon mayonnaise on each steak, sprinkle with 1 teaspoon mustard, top with some slices of onion and lettuce and then serve.

Nutrition:

Calories – 305
Fat – 19 g
Protein – 7 g
Carbohydrates – 28 g
Fiber – 3.6 g

Salad With Vinaigrette

Preparation Time: 25 minutes

Cooking Time: 0 minutes

Servings: 4

Ingredients

Olive oil – ½ cup

Balsamic vinegar - 4 Tbsps.

Chopped fresh oregano – 2 Tbsps.

Pinch red pepper flakes

Ground black pepper

Shredded green leaf lettuce – 4 cups

Carrot – 1, shredded

Fresh green beans – ¾ cup, cut into 1-inch pieces

Large radishes – 3, sliced thin

Directions:

To make the vinaigrette: put the vinaigrette ingredients in a bowl and whisk.

To make the salad, in a bowl, toss together the carrot, lettuce, green beans, and radishes.

Add the vinaigrette to the vegetables and toss to coat. Arrange the salad on plates and serve.

Nutrition:

Calories: 273

Fat: 27g

Carb: 7g

Phosphorus: 30mg

Potassium: 197mg

Sodium: 27mg

Protein: 1g

Salad With Lemon Dressing

Preparation Time: 10 minutes
Cooking Time: 0 minutes
Servings: 4
Ingredients
Heavy cream – ¼ cup
Freshly squeezed lemon juice – ¼ cup
Granulated sugar – 2 Tbsps.
Chopped fresh dill – 2 Tbsps.
Finely chopped scallion – 2 Tbsps. green part only
Ground black pepper – ¼ tsp.
English cucumber – 1, sliced thin
Shredded green cabbage – 2 cups

Directions:

In a small bowl, stir together the lemon juice, cream, sugar, dill, scallion, and pepper until well blended.

In a large bowl, toss together the cucumber and cabbage.

Place the salad in the refrigerator and chill for 1 hour.

Stir before serving.

Nutrition:

Calories: 99
Fat: 6g
Carb: 13g
Phosphorus: 38mg
Potassium: 200mg
Sodium: 14mg
Protein: 2g

Shrimp With Salsa

Preparation Time: 15 minutes
Cooking Time: 10 minutes
Servings: 4
Ingredients
Olive oil – 2 Tbsp.
Large shrimp – 6 ounces, peeled and deveined, tails left on
Minced garlic – 1 tsp.
Chopped English cucumber – ½ cup
Chopped mango – ½ cup
Zest of 1 lime
Juice of 1 lime
Ground black pepper
Lime wedges for garnish
Directions:
Soak 4 wooden skewers in water for 30 minutes.
Preheat the barbecue to medium heat.
In a bowl, toss together the olive oil, shrimp, and garlic.
Thread the shrimp onto the skewers, about 4 shrimp per skewer.
In a bowl, stir together the mango, cucumber, lime zest, and lime juice, and season the salsa lightly with pepper. Set aside.
Grill the shrimp for 10 minutes, turning once or until the shrimp is opaque and cooked through.
Season the shrimp lightly with pepper.
Serve the shrimp on the cucumber salsa with lime wedges on the side.
Nutrition:
Calories: 120
Fat: 8g
Carb: 4g
Phosphorus: 91mg
Potassium: 129mg
Sodium: 60mg
Protein: 9g

Cauliflower Soup

Preparation Time: 20 minutes
Cooking Time: 30 minutes
Servings: 6
Ingredients
Unsalted butter – 1 tsp.
Sweet onion – 1 small, chopped
Minced garlic – 2 tsps.
Small head cauliflower – 1, cut into small florets
Curry powder – 2 tsps.
Water to cover the cauliflower
Light sour cream – ½ cup
Chopped fresh cilantro – 3 Tbsps.
Directions:
In a large saucepan, heat the butter over a medium-high heat and sauté the onion-garlic for about 3 minutes or until softened.

Add the cauliflower, water, and curry powder.

Bring the soup to a boil, then reduce the heat to low and simmer for 20 minutes or until the cauliflower is tender.

Puree the soup until creamy and smooth with a hand mixer.

Transfer the soup back into a saucepan and stir in the sour cream and cilantro.

Heat the soup on medium heat for 5 minutes or until warmed through.
Nutrition:
Calories: 33
Fat: 2g
Carb: 4g
Phosphorus: 30mg
Potassium: 167mg
Sodium: 22mg
Protein: 1g

Cabbage Stew

Preparation Time: 20 minutes
Cooking Time: 35 minutes
Servings: 6

Ingredients

Unsalted butter – 1 tsp.

Large sweet onion - ½, chopped

Minced garlic – 1 tsp.

Shredded green cabbage – 6 cups

Celery stalks - 3, chopped with leafy tops

Scallion – 1, both green and white parts, chopped

Chopped fresh parsley – 2 Tbsps.

Freshly squeezed lemon juice – 2 Tbsps.

Chopped fresh thyme – 1 Tbsp.

Chopped savory – 1 tsp.

Chopped fresh oregano – 1 tsp.

Water

Fresh green beans – 1 cup, cut into 1-inch pieces

Ground black pepper

Directions:

Melt the butter in a pot.

Sauté the onion and garlic in the melted butter for 3 minutes, or until the vegetables are softened.

Add the celery, cabbage, scallion, parsley, lemon juice, thyme, savory, and oregano to the pot, add enough water to cover the vegetables by 4 inches.

Bring the soup to a boil. Reduce the heat to low and simmer the soup for 25 minutes or until the vegetables are tender.

Add the green beans and simmer for 3 minutes.

Season with pepper.

Nutrition:
Calories: 33
Fat: 1g
Carb: 6g
Phosphorus: 29mg
Potassium: 187mg
Sodium: 20mg
Protein: 1g

Baked Haddock

Preparation Time: 10 minutes

Cooking Time: 20 minutes

Servings: 4

Ingredients

Bread crumbs – ½ cup

Chopped fresh parsley – 3 Tbsps.

Lemon zest – 1 Tbsp.

Chopped fresh thyme – 1 tsp.

Ground black pepper – ¼ tsp.

Melted unsalted butter – 1 Tbsp.

Haddock fillets – 12-ounces, deboned and skinned

Directions:

Preheat the oven to 350F.

In a bowl, stir together the parsley, breadcrumbs, lemon zest, thyme, and pepper until well combined.

Add the melted butter and toss until the mixture resembles coarse crumbs.

Place the haddock on a baking sheet and spoon the bread crumb mixture on top, pressing down firmly.

Bake the haddock in the oven for 20 minutes or until the fish is just cooked through and flakes off in chunks when pressed.

Nutrition:

Calories: 143

Fat: 4g

Carb: 10g

Phosphorus: 216mg

Potassium: 285mg

Sodium: 281mg

Protein: 16g

Herbed Chicken

Preparation Time: 20 minutes
Cooking Time: 15 minutes
Servings: 4

Ingredients

Boneless, skinless chicken breast – 12 ounces, cut into 8 strips

Egg white – 1

Water – 2 Tbsps. divided

Breadcrumbs – ½ cup

Unsalted butter – ¼ cup, divided

Juice of 1 lemon

Zest of 1 lemon

Fresh chopped basil – 1 Tbsp.

Fresh chopped thyme – 1 tsp.

Lemon slices, for garnish

Directions:

Place the chicken strips between 2 sheets of plastic wrap and pound each flat with a rolling pin.

In a bowl, whisk together the egg and 1 tbsp. water.

Put the breadcrumbs in another bowl.

Dredge the chicken strips, one at a time, in the egg, then the breadcrumbs and set the breaded strips aside on a plate.

In a large skillet over medium heat, melt 2 tbsps. of the butter.

Cook the strips in the butter for 3 minutes, turning once, or until they are golden and cooked through. Transfer the chicken to a plate.

Add the lemon zest, lemon juice, basil, thyme, and remaining 1 tbsp. water to the skillet and stir until the mixture simmers.

Remove the sauce from the heat and stir in the remaining 2 tbsps. butter.

Serve the chicken with the lemon sauce drizzled over the top and garnished with lemon slices.

Nutrition:
Calories: 255
Fat: 14g
Carb: 11g
Phosphorus: 180mg
Potassium: 321mg
Sodium: 261mg
Protein: 20g

Pesto Pork Chops

Preparation Time: 20 minutes
Cooking Time: 20 minutes
Servings: 4
Ingredients
Pork top-loin chops – 4 (3-ounce) boneless, fat trimmed
Herb pesto – 8 tsps.
Breadcrumbs – ½ cup
Olive oil – 1 Tbsp.
Directions:
Preheat the oven to 450F.
Line a baking sheet with foil. Set aside.
Rub 1 tsp. of pesto evenly over both sides of each pork chop.
Lightly dredge each pork chop in the breadcrumbs.
Heat the oil in a skillet.
Brown the pork chops on each side for 5 minutes.
Place the pork chops on the baking sheet.
Bake for 10 minutes or until pork reaches 145F in the center.

Nutrition:
Calories: 210
Fat: 7g
Carb: 10g
Phosphorus: 179mg
Potassium: 220mg
Sodium: 148mg
Protein: 24g

Vegetable Curry

Preparation Time: 15 minutes
Cooking Time: 45 minutes
Servings: 4
Ingredients
Olive oil – 2 tsps.
Sweet onion – ½, diced
Minced garlic – 2 tsps.
Grated fresh ginger – 2 tsps.
Eggplant – ½, peeled and diced
Carrot – 1, peeled and diced
Red bell pepper – 1, diced
Hot curry powder – 1 Tbsp.
Ground cumin – 1 tsp.
Coriander – ½ tsp.
Pinch cayenne pepper
Homemade vegetable stock – 1 ½ cups
Cornstarch – 1 Tbsp.
Water – ¼ cup

Directions:
Heat the oil in a stockpot.
Sauté the ginger, garlic, and onion for 3 minutes or until they are softened.
Add the red pepper, carrots, eggplant, and stir often for 6 minutes.
Stir in the cumin, curry powder, coriander, cayenne pepper, and vegetable stock.
Bring the curry to a boil and then lower the heat to low.
Simmer the curry for 30 minutes or until the vegetables are tender.
In a bowl, stir together the cornstarch and water.
Stir in the cornstarch mixture into the curry and simmer for 5 minutes or until the sauce has thickened.

Nutrition:
Calories: 100
Fat: 3g
Carb: 9g
Phosphorus: 28mg
Potassium: 180mg
Sodium: 218mg
Protein: 1g

Grilled Steak With Salsa

Preparation Time: 20 minutes
Cooking Time: 15 minutes
Servings: 4
Ingredients for the salsa
Chopped English cucumber - 1 cup
Boiled and diced red bell pepper – ¼ cup
Scallion – 1, both green and white parts, chopped
Chopped fresh cilantro – 2 Tbsps.
Juice of 1 lime
For the steak
Beef tenderloin steaks – 4 (3-ounce), room temperature
Olive oil
Freshly ground black pepper

Directions:
To make the salsa, in a bowl, combine the lime juice, cilantro, scallion, bell pepper, and cucumber. Set aside.

To make the steak: Preheat a barbecue to medium heat.

Rub the steaks all over with oil and season with pepper.

Grill the steaks for about 5 minutes per side for medium-rare, or until the desired doneness.

Serve the steaks topped with salsa.

Nutrition:
Calories: 130
Fat: 6g
Carb: 1g
Phosphorus: 186mg
Potassium: 272mg
Sodium: 39mg
Protein: 19g

Parsley Root Veg Stew

Preparation Time: 5 minutes
Cooking Time: 35-40 minutes
Servings:4
Ingredients:

2 garlic cloves

2 cups white rice

1 tsp. ground cumin

1 diced onion

2 cups water

4 peeled and diced turnips

1 tsp. cayenne pepper

¼ cup chopped fresh parsley

½ tsp. ground cinnamon

2 tbsps. olive oil

1 tsp. ground ginger

2 peeled and diced carrots

Directions:

In a large pot, heat the oil on a medium high heat before sautéing the onion for 4-5 minutes until soft.

Add the turnips and cook for 10 minutes or until golden brown.

Add the garlic, cumin, ginger, cinnamon, and cayenne pepper, cooking for a further 3 minutes.

Add the carrots and stock to the pot and then bring to the boil.

Turn the heat down to medium heat, cover and simmer for 20 minutes.

Meanwhile add the rice to a pot of water and bring to the boil.

Turn down to simmer for 15 minutes.

Drain and place the lid on for 5 minutes to steam.

Garnish the root vegetable stew with parsley to serve alongside the rice.

Nutrition:

Calories 210, Protein 4 g, Carbs 32 g, Fat 7 g

Mixed Pepper Paella

Preparation Time: 10 minutes
Cooking Time: 35-40 minutes
Servings: 2
Ingredients:

1 tbsp. extra virgin olive oil

½ chopped red onion

1 lemon

½ chopped yellow bell pepper

1 cup homemade chicken broth

½ chopped zucchini

1 tsp. dried oregano

½ chopped red bell pepper

1 tsp. dried parsley

1 cup brown rice

1 tsp. paprika

Directions:

Add the rice to a pot of cold water and cook for 15 minutes.

Drain the water, cover the pan and leave to one side.

Heat the oil in a skillet over medium-high heat.

Add the bell peppers, onion and zucchini, sautéing for 5 minutes.

To the pan, add the rice, herbs, spices and juice of the lemon along with the chicken broth.

Cover and turn the heat right down and allow to simmer for 15-20 minutes.

Serve hot.

Nutrition:

Calories 210, Protein 4 g, Carbs 33 g, Fat 7 g,

Cauliflower Rice & Runny Eggs

Preparation Time: 5 minutes
Cooking Time: 30 minutes
Servings:4
Ingredients:

4 eggs

1 tbsp. extra virgin olive oil

1 tsp. black pepper

1 tbsp. chopped fresh chives

2 cups cauliflower

1 tbsp. curry powder

Directions:

Preheat the oven to 375°F/Gas Mark 5.

Soak the cauliflower in warm water in advance if possible.

Grate or chop into rice-size pieces.

Bring the cauliflower to the boil in a pot of water and then turn down to simmer for 7 minutes.

Drain completely.

Place on a baking tray and sprinkle over curry powder and black pepper - toss to coat.

Bake in the oven for 20 minutes, stirring occasionally.

Meanwhile, boil a separate pan of water and add the eggs for 7 minutes.

Run under the cold tap, crack and peel the eggs before cutting in half.

Top the cauliflower with eggs and chopped chives.

Serve hot!

Nutrition:

Calories 120, Protein 7 g, Carbs 4 g, Fat 8 g,

Minted Zucchini Noodles

Preparation Time: 5 minutes
Cooking Time: 10 minutes
Servings: 2
Ingredients:

¼ deseeded and chopped red chili

2 tbsps. Extra virgin olive oil

½ juiced lemon

4 peeled and sliced zucchinis

½ cup chopped fresh mint

1 tsp. black pepper

½ cup arugula

Directions:

Whisk the mint, pepper, chili and olive oil to make a dressing.

Meanwhile, heat a pan of water on a high heat and bring to the boil.

Add the zucchini noodles and turn the heat down to simmer for 3-4 minutes.

Remove from the heat and place in a bowl of cold water immediately.

Toss the noodles in the dressing.

Mix the arugula with the lemon juice to serve on the top.

Enjoy!

Nutrition:

Calories 148, Protein 2 g, Carbs 4 g, Fat 13 g

Chili Tempeh & Scallions

Preparation Time: 10 minutes
Cooking Time: 15 minutes
Servings:2
Ingredients:

½ cup chopped scallions

1 juiced lime

1 tsp. soy sauce

2 oz. cubed tempeh

1 tbsp. grated ginger

1 tsp. coconut oil

½ deseeded and chopped red chili

Directions:

Mix the oil, soy sauce, chili flakes, lime juice and ginger together.

Marinate the tempeh in this for as long as possible.

Preheat the broiler to medium heat.

Add tempeh to a lined baking tray and broil for 10-15 minutes or until hot through.

Remove and sprinkle with scallions to serve.

Nutrition:

Calories 221, Protein 6 g, Carbs 8 g, Fat 10 g

Dinner Recipes

Pork Chili

Preparation Time: 15 minutes
Cooking Time: 1 hour
Servings: 8
Ingredients:
2 tablespoons extra-virgin organic olive oil
2-pound ground pork
1 medium red bell pepper, seeded and chopped
1 medium onion, chopped
5 garlic cloves, chopped finely
1 (2-inch) part of hot pepper, minced
1 tablespoon ground cumin
1 teaspoon ground turmeric
3 tablespoon chili powder
½ teaspoon chipotle chili powder
Salt and freshly ground black pepper, to taste
1 cup chicken broth
1 (28-ounce) can fire-roasted crushed tomatoes
2 medium Bok choy heads, sliced
1 avocado, peeled, pitted and chopped
Directions:
In a sizable pan, heat oil on medium heat.
Add pork and stir fry for about 5 minutes.
Add bell pepper, onion, garlic, hot pepper and spices and stir fry for approximately 5 minutes.
Add broth and tomatoes and convey with a boil.
Stir in Bok choy and cook, covered for approximately twenty minutes.
Uncover and cook approximately 20-half an hour.
Serve hot while using topping of avocado.
Nutrition:
Calories: 402, Fat: 9g, Carbohydrates: 18g, Fiber: 6g, Protein: 32g

Ground Pork With Water Chestnuts

Preparation Time: fifteen minutes
Cooking Time: 12 minutes
Servings: 4
Ingredients:

1 tablespoon plus 1 teaspoon coconut oil

1 tablespoon fresh ginger, minced

1 bunch scallion (white and green parts separated), chopped

1-pound lean ground pork

Salt, to taste

1 tablespoon 5-spice powder

1 (18-ounce) can water chestnuts, drained and chopped

1 tablespoon organic honey

2 tablespoons fresh lime juice

Directions:

In a big heavy bottomed skillet, heat oil on high heat.

Add ginger and scallion whites and sauté for approximately ½-1½ minutes.

Add pork and cook for approximately 4-5 minutes.

Drain the extra Fat from skillet.

Add salt and 5-spice powder and cook for approximately 2-3 minutes.

Add scallion greens and remaining ingredients and cook, stirring continuously for about 1-2 minutes.

Nutrition:

Calories: 520, Fat: 30g, Carbohydrates: 37g, Fiber: 4g, Protein: 25g

Glazed Pork Chops With Peach

Preparation Time: 15 minutes
Cooking Time: 16 minutes
Servings: 2
Ingredients:

2 boneless pork chops

Salt and freshly ground black pepper, to taste

1 ripe yellow peach, peeled, pitted, chopped and divided

1 tbsp organic olive oil

2 tablespoons shallot, minced

2 tablespoons garlic, minced

2 tablespoons fresh ginger, minced

1 tablespoon organic honey

1 tablespoon balsamic vinegar

1 tablespoon coconut aminos

¼ teaspoon red pepper flakes, crushed

¼ cup water

Directions:

Sprinkle the pork chops with salt and black pepper generously.

In a blender, add 1 / 2 of peach and pulse till a puree form.

Reserve remaining peach.

In a skillet, heat oil on medium heat.

Add shallots and sauté approximately 1-2 minutes.

Add garlic and ginger and sauté approximately 1 minute.

Add remaining ingredients and lower heat to medium-low.

Bring to your boil and simmer for approximately 4-5 minutes or till a sticky glaze form.

Remove from heat and reserve 1/3 with the glaze and keep aside.

Coat the chops with remaining glaze.

Heat a nonstick skillet on medium-high heat.

Add chops and sear for around 4 minutes from both sides.

Transfer the chops in a plate and coat with all the remaining glaze evenly.

Top with reserved chopped peach and serve.

Nutrition:

Calories: 446, Fat: 20g, Carbohydrates: 26g, Fiber: 5g, Protein: 38g

Pork Chops In Creamy Sauce

Preparation Time: fifteen minutes
Cooking Time: 14 minutes
Servings: 4
Ingredients:

2 garlic cloves, chopped

1 small jalapeño pepper, chopped

¼ cup fresh cilantro leaves

1½ teaspoons ground turmeric, divided

1 tablespoon fish sauce

2 tablespoons fresh lime juice

1 (13½-ounce) can coconut milk

4 (½-inch thick) pork chops

Salt, to taste

1 tablespoon coconut oil

1 shallot, chopped finely

Directions:

In a blender, add garlic, jalapeño pepper, cilantro, 1 teaspoon of ground turmeric, fish sauce, lime juice and coconut milk and pulse till smooth.

Sprinkle the pork with salt and remaining turmeric evenly.

In a skillet, melt butter on medium-high heat.

Add shallots and sauté approximately 1 minute.

Add chops and cook for approximately 2 minutes per side.

Transfer the chops inside a bowl.

Add coconut mixture and convey to your boil.

Reduce heat to medium and simmer, stirring occasionally for approximately 5 minutes.

Stir in pork chops and cook for about 3-4 minutes.

Serve hot.

Nutrition:

Calories: 437, Fat: 9g, Carbohydrates: 21g, Fiber: 4g, Protein: 38g

Baked Pork & Mushroom Meatballs

Preparation Time: 15 minutes
Cooking Time: fifteen minutes
Servings: 6
Ingredients:

1-pound lean ground pork

1 organic egg white, beaten

4 fresh shiitake mushrooms, stemmed and minced

1 tablespoon fresh parsley, minced

1 tablespoon fresh basil leaves, minced

1 tablespoon fresh mint leaves, minced

2 teaspoons fresh lemon zest, grated finely

1½ teaspoons fresh ginger, grated finely

Salt and freshly ground black pepper, to taste

Directions:

Preheat the oven to 425 degrees F. Arrange the rack inside center of oven.

Line a baking sheet with a parchment paper.

In a sizable bowl, add all ingredients and mix till well combined.

Make small equal-sized balls from mixture.

Arrange the balls onto prepared baking sheet in a single layer.

Bake for approximately 12-15 minutes or till done completely.

Nutrition:

Calories: 411, Fat: 19g, Carbohydrates: 27g, Fiber: 11g, Protein: 35g

Butternut Squash, Kale And Ground Beef Breakfast Bowl

Preparation Time: 10 minutes
Cooking Time: 20 minutes
Serving: 3
Ingredients:
¼ cup coconut milk
1 to 2 tbsp coconut shavings
¼ tsp ground cinnamon
¼ tsp ground ginger
½ tsp spicy curry
1 tsp garam masala
¼ large butternut squash, cook and peeled
5 kale leaves, chopped
Salt and pepper to taste
¼-lb lean grass-fed beef
1 to 2 chopped button mushrooms
½ of small onion, diced
Coconut oil

Directions:
In a skillet, heat a small amount of coconut oil over medium high heat. Sauté the mushroom and onions. Add the salt and pepper. Continue cooking for three minutes.

Add the ground beef, curry, garam masala, cinnamon and ginger. Continue to cook until the beef turns brown.

Add the chopped kale and cook until the leaves wilt.

Stir in the coconut milk and add the cooked squash. Continue cooking until the squash breaks down.

Transfer in a bowl and garnish with coconut shavings. Serve warm.

Nutrition:
Calories 225, Total Fat 14g, Saturated Fat 3g, Total Carbs 17g, Net Carbs 13g, Protein 10g, Sugar: 6g, Fiber 4g, Sodium 43mg, Potassium 469mg

Light Beef Soup

Preparation Time: 10 minutes
Cooking Time: 1 hour and 10 minutes
Serving: 8
Ingredients:
1 tablespoon olive oil

1 large onion, chopped

2 cloves of garlic, minced

2 stalks celery, sliced

1-pound beef chuck, bones removed and cut into cubes

salt and pepper to taste

2 carrots, peeled and diced

8 ounces mushrooms, sliced

½ teaspoon dried thyme

2 cups beef broth

2 cups chicken broth

2 cups water

1 bay leaf
Directions:
Heat the oil in a pot and sauté the onion, garlic, and celery until fragrant.

Stir in the beef chuck and season with salt and pepper.

Add the rest of the ingredients.

Close the lid and bring to a boil.

Allow to simmer for 60 minutes until the beef is soft.

Serve and enjoy.
Nutrition:
Calories 117, Total Fat 5g, Saturated Fat 1g, Total Carbs 5g, Net Carbs 4g, Protein 13g, Sugar: 2g, Fiber 1g, Sodium 546mg, Potassium 409mg

Beef Noodle Soup

Preparation Time: 20 minutes
Cooking Time: 25 minutes
Serving: 4
Ingredients:

4 cups zucchini, spiral

1 cup carrots, spiral

1 cup jicama, spiral

2 pcs Beef Knorr Cubes

8 cups water

freshly ground pepper to taste

3 stalks green onions, chopped

¼ lb beef, thinly sliced

4 tbsp ground pork rinds (chicharon), divided

2 hardboiled eggs, halved

1 tsp salt

Directions:

In a pot, bring water to a boil. Add Knorr cubes and fish sauce.

With a strainer, dip into the boiling water the zucchini noodles and cook for 3 minutes. Remove from water, drain and arrange into 4 bowls. If needed, you can cook zucchini noodles in batches.

Then, cook the carrots in the boiling pot of water using a strainer still. Around 2-3 minutes, drain and arrange on top of the zucchini noodles.

Do the same with jicama, cook in the pot, drain and arrange equally into the bowls.

Do same for the thinly sliced beef. Cook for 5-10 minutes in the boiling pot of soup, swirling the strainer occasionally to ensure uniform cooking for the beef. Arrange equally on the 4 bowls.

Sprinkle 1 tbsp of ground pork rinds on each bowl, topped by chopped green onions, ½ hardboiled egg and freshly ground pepper.

Taste the boiling pot of soup and adjust to your taste. It should be slightly saltier than the usual so that the noodles will absorb the excess salt once you pour it into the bowls. Add more fish sauce to make it salty or add water to make the pot less salty. Keep soup on a rolling boil before pouring 1-2 cups of soup on each bowl. Serve right away.

Nutrition:

Calories 101, Total Fat 4g, Saturated Fat 1g, Total Carbs 7g, Net Carbs g, Protein 10g, Sugar: 3g, Fiber 3g, Sodium 1100mg, Potassium 353mg

Spanish Rice Casserole With Beef

Preparation Time: 10 minutes
Cooking Time: 25 minutes
Serving: 2
Ingredients:
2 tablespoons chopped green bell pepper
1/4 teaspoon Worcestershire sauce
1/4 teaspoon ground cumin
1/4 cup finely chopped onion
1/4 cup chile sauce
1/3 cup uncooked long grain, brown rice
1/2-pound lean ground beef
1/2 teaspoon salt
1/2 teaspoon brown sugar
1/2 pinch ground black pepper
1/2 cup water
1/2 (14.5 ounce) can canned tomatoes
1 tablespoon chopped fresh cilantro
Directions:
Place a nonstick saucepan on medium fire and brown beef for 10 minutes while crumbling beef. Discard fat.

Stir in pepper, Worcestershire sauce, cumin, brown sugar, salt, chile sauce, rice, water, tomatoes, green bell pepper, and onion. Mix well and cook for 10 minutes until blended and a bit tender.

Transfer to an ovenproof casserole and press down firmly. Broil for 3 minutes until top is lightly browned.

Serve and enjoy with chopped cilantro.

Nutrition:

Calories 437, Total Fat 16g, Saturated Fat 2.5g, Total Carbs 38g, Net Carbs 30g, Protein 38g, Sugar: 12g, Fiber 8g, Sodium 1144mg, Potassium 1235mg

Kefta Styled Beef Patties With Cucumber Salad

Preparation Time: 10 minutes
Cooking Time: 10 minutes
Serving: 4
Ingredients:

2 pcs of 6-inch pita, quartered

½ tsp freshly ground black pepper

1 tbsp fresh lemon juice

½ cup plain Greek yogurt, fat free

2 cups thinly sliced English cucumber

½ tsp ground cinnamon

½ tsp salt

1 tsp ground cumin

2 tsp ground coriander

1 tbsp peeled and chopped ginger

¼ cup cilantro, fresh

¼ cup plus 2 tbsp fresh parsley, chopped and divided

1 lb. ground sirloin

Directions:

On medium high fire, preheat a grill pan coated with cooking spray.

In a medium bowl, mix together cinnamon, salt, cumin, coriander, ginger, cilantro, parsley and beef. Then divide the mixture equally into four parts and shaping each portion into a patty ½ inch thick.

Then place patties on pan cooking each side for three minutes or until desired doneness is achieved.

In a separate bowl, toss together vinegar and cucumber.

In a small bowl, whisk together pepper, juice, 2 tbsp parsley and yogurt.

Serve each patty on a plate with ½ cup cucumber mixture and 2 tbsp of the yogurt sauce.

Nutrition Facts Per Serving

Calories 306, Total Fat 13g, Saturated Fat 2g, Total Carbs 11g, Net Carbs 9g, Protein 34g, Sugar: 2g, Fiber 2g, Sodium 433mg, Potassium 507mg

Broiled Lamb Shoulder

Preparation Time: 10 minutes
Cooking Time: 8-10 minutes
Servings: 10
Ingredients:

2 tablespoons fresh ginger, minced

2 tablespoons garlic, minced

¼ cup fresh lemongrass stalk, minced

¼ cup fresh orange juice

¼ cup coconut aminos

Freshly ground black pepper, to taste

2-pound lamb shoulder, trimmed

Directions:

In a bowl, mix together all ingredients except lamb shoulder.

In a baking dish, squeeze lamb shoulder and coat the lamb with half in the marinade mixture generously.

Reserve remaining mixture.

Refrigerate to marinate for overnight.

Preheat the broiler of oven. Place a rack inside a broiler pan and arrange about 4-5-inches from heating unit.

Remove lamb shoulder from refrigerator and remove excess marinade.

Broil approximately 4-5 minutes from both sides.

Serve with all the reserved marinade like a sauce.

Nutrition:

Calories: 250, Fat: 19g, Carbohydrates: 2g. Fiber: 0g, Protein: 15g

Pan-Seared Lamb Chops

Preparation Time: 10 minutes
Cooking Time: 4-6 minutes
Servings: 4
Ingredients:

4 garlic cloves, peeled

Salt, to taste

1 teaspoon black mustard seeds, crushed finely

2 teaspoons ground cumin

1 teaspoon ground ginger

1 teaspoon ground coriander

½ teaspoon ground cinnamon

Freshly ground black pepper, to taste

1 tablespoon coconut oil

8 medium lamb chops, trimmed

Directions:

Place garlic cloves onto a cutting board and sprinkle with salt.

With a knife, crush the garlic till a paste form.

In a bowl, mix together garlic paste and spices.

With a clear, crisp knife, make 3-4 cuts on both side in the chops.

Rub the chops with garlic mixture generously.

In a large skillet, melt butter on medium heat.

Add chops and cook for approximately 2-3 minutes per side or till desired doneness.

Nutrition:

Calories: 443, Fat: 11g, Carbohydrates: 27g, Fiber: 4g, Protein: 40g

Roasted Lamb Chops With Relish

Preparation Time: 15 minutes
Cooking Time: half an hour
Servings: 4
Ingredients:
For Lamb Marinade:
4 garlic cloves, chopped
1 (2-inch) piece fresh ginger, chopped
2 green chilies, seeded and chopped
1 teaspoon fresh lime zest
2 teaspoons garam masala
1 teaspoon ground coriander
1 teaspoon ground cumin
½ teaspoon ground cinnamon
1 teaspoon coconut oil, melted
2 tablespoons fresh lime juice
6-7 tablespoons plain Greek yogurt
1 (8-bone) rack of lamb, trimmed
2 onions, sliced
For Relish:
½ of garlic herb, chopped
1 (1-inch) piece fresh ginger, chopped
¼ cup fresh cilantro, chopped
¼ cup fresh mint, chopped
1 green chili, seeded and chopped
1 teaspoon fresh lime zest
1 teaspoon organic honey
2 tablespoons fresh apple juice
2 tablespoons fresh lime juice

Directions:

For chops in a very mixer, add all ingredients except yogurt, chops and onions and pulse till smooth.

Transfer the mixture in a large bowl with yogurt and stir to combine well.

Add chops and coat with mixture generously.

Refrigerate to marinate for approximately 24 hours.

Preheat the oven to 375 degrees F. Linea roasting pan with a foil paper.

Place the onion wedges in the bottom of prepared roasting pan.

Arrange rack of lamb over onion wedges.

Roast approximately half an hour.

Meanwhile for relish in the blender, add all ingredients and pulse till smooth.

Serve chops and onions alongside relish.

Nutrition:

Calories: 439, Fat: 17g, Carbohydrates: 26g, Fiber: 10g, Protein: 41g

Grilled Lamb Chops

Preparation Time: 10 min
Cooking Time: 6 minutes
Servings: 4
Ingredients:

1 tablespoon fresh ginger, grated

4 garlic cloves, chopped roughly

1 teaspoon ground cumin

½ teaspoon red chili powder

Salt and freshly ground black pepper, to taste

1 tbsp essential olive oil

1 tablespoon fresh lemon juice

8 lamb chops, trimmed

Directions:

In a bowl, mix together all ingredients except chops.

With a hand blender, blend till a smooth mixture form.

Add chops and coat with mixture generously.

Refrigerate to marinate for overnight.

Preheat the barbecue grill till hot. Grease the grill grate.

Grill the chops for approximately 3 minutes per side.

Nutrition:

Calories: 227, Fat: 12g, Carbohydrates: 1g, Fiber: 0g, Protein: 30g

Lamb Burgers With Avocado Dip

Preparation Time: 20 minutes
Cooking Time: 10 minutes
Servings: 4-6
Ingredients:
For Burgers:
1 (2-inch) piece fresh ginger, grated
1-pound lean ground lamb
1 medium onion, grated
2 minced garlic cloves
1 bunch fresh mint leaves, chopped finely
2 teaspoons ground coriander
2 teaspoons ground cumin
½ teaspoon ground allspice
½ teaspoon ground cinnamon
Salt and freshly ground black pepper, to taste
1 tbsp essential olive oil
For Dip:
3 small cucumbers, peeled and grated
1 avocado, peeled, pitted and chopped
½ of garlic oil, crushed
2 tablespoons fresh lemon juice
2 tablespoons olive oil
2 tablespoons fresh dill, chopped finely
2 tablespoons chives, chopped finely
Salt and freshly ground black pepper, to taste
Directions:
Preheat the broiler of oven. Lightly, grease a broiler pan.
For burgers in a big bowl, squeeze the juice of ginger.
Add remaining ingredients and mix till well combined.
Make equal sized burgers from your mixture.
Arrange the burgers in broiler pan and broil approximately 5 minutes per side.
Meanwhile for dip squeeze the cucumbers juice in a bowl.

In a blender, add avocado, garlic, lemon juice and oil and pulse till smooth.

Transfer the avocado mixture in a bowl.

Add remaining ingredients and stir to mix.

Serve the burgers with avocado dip.

Nutrition:

Calories: 462, Fat: 15g, Carbohydrates: 23g, Fiber: 9g, Protein: 39g

Lamb & Pineapple Kebabs

Preparation Time: 15 minutes

Cooking Time: 10 minutes

Servings: 4-6

Ingredients:

1 large pineapple, cubed into 1½-inch size, divided

1 (½-inch) piece fresh ginger, chopped

2 garlic cloves, chopped

Salt, to taste

16-24-ounce lamb shoulder steak, trimmed and cubed into 1½-inch size

Fresh mint leaves coming from a bunch

Ground cinnamon, to taste

Directions:

In a blender, add about 1½ of pineapple, ginger, garlic and salt and pulse till smooth.

Transfer the amalgamation right into a large bowl.

Add chops and coat with mixture generously.

Refrigerate to marinate for about 1-2 hours.

Preheat the grill to medium heat. Grease the grill grate.

Thread lam, remaining pineapple and mint leaves onto pre-soaked wooden skewers.

Grill the kebabs approximately 10 min, turning occasionally.

Nutrition:

Calories: 482, Fat: 16g, Carbohydrates: 22g, Fiber: 5g, Protein: 377g

Baked Meatballs & Scallions

Preparation Time: 20 min
Cooking Time: 35 minutes
Servings: 4-6
Ingredients:
For Meatballs:
1 lemongrass stalk, outer skin peeled and chopped
1 (1½-inch) piece fresh ginger, sliced
3 garlic cloves, chopped
1 cup fresh cilantro leaves, chopped roughly
½ cup fresh basil leaves, chopped roughly
2 tablespoons plus 1 teaspoon fish sauce
2 tablespoons water
2 tablespoons fresh lime juice
½ pound lean ground pork
1-pound lean ground lamb
1 carrot, peeled and grated
1 organic egg, beaten
For Scallions:
16 stalks scallions, trimmed
2 tablespoons coconut oil, melted
Salt, to taste
½ cup water
Directions:
Preheat the oven to 375 degrees F. Grease a baking dish.

In a blender, add lemongrass, ginger, garlic, fresh herbs, fish sauce, water and lime juice and pulse till chopped finely.

Transfer the amalgamation in a bowl with remaining ingredients and mix till well combined.

Make about 1-inch balls from mixture.

Arrange the balls into prepared baking dish in a single layer.

In another rimmed baking dish, arrange scallion stalks in a very single layer.

Drizzle with coconut oil and sprinkle with salt.

Pour water in the baking dish and with a foil paper cover it tightly.

Bake the scallion for around a half-hour.

Bake the meatballs for approximately 30-35 minutes.

Nutrition:

Calories: 432, Fat: 13g, Carbohydrates: 25g, Fiber: 8g, Protein: 40g

Pork With Bell Pepper

Preparation Time: 15 minutes
Cooking Time: 13 minutes
Servings: 4
Ingredients:

1 tablespoon fresh ginger, chopped finely

4 garlic cloves, chopped finely

1 cup fresh cilantro, chopped and divided

¼ cup plus 1 tbsp olive oil, divided

1-pound tender pork, trimmed, sliced thinly

2 onions, sliced thinly

1 green bell pepper, seeded and sliced thinly

1 tablespoon fresh lime juice

Directions:

In a substantial bowl, mix together ginger, garlic, ½ cup of cilantro and ¼ cup of oil.

Add pork and coat with mixture generously.

Refrigerate to marinate approximately a couple of hours.

Heat a big skillet on medium-high heat.

Add pork mixture and stir fry for approximately 4-5 minutes.

Transfer the pork right into a bowl.

In the same skillet, heat remaining oil on medium heat.

Add onion and sauté for approximately 3 minutes.

Stir in bell pepper and stir fry for about 3 minutes.

Stir in pork, lime juice and remaining cilantro and cook for about 2 minutes.

Serve hot.

Nutrition:

Calories: 429, Fat: 19g, Carbohydrates: 26g, Fiber: 9g, Protein: 35g

Pork With Pineapple

Preparation Time: 15 minutes
Cooking Time: 14 minutes
Servings: 4
Ingredients:

2 tablespoons coconut oil

1½ pound pork tenderloin, trimmed and cut into bite-sized pieces

1 onion, chopped

2 minced garlic cloves

1 (1-inch) piece fresh ginger, minced

20-ounce pineapple, cut into chunks

1 large red bell pepper, seeded and chopped

¼ cup fresh pineapple juice

¼ cup coconut aminos

Salt and freshly ground black pepper, to taste

Directions:

In a substantial skillet, melt coconut oil on high heat.

Add pork and stir fry approximately 4-5 minutes.

Transfer the pork right into a bowl.

In exactly the same skillet, heat remaining oil on medium heat.

Add onion, garlic and ginger and sauté for around 2 minutes.

Stir in pineapple and bell pepper and stir fry for around 3 minutes.

Stir in pork, pineapple juice and coconut aminos and cook for around 3-4 minutes.

Serve hot.

Nutrition:

Calories: 431, Fat: 10g, Carbohydrates: 22g, Fiber: 8g, Protein: 33g

Spiced Pork

Preparation Time: fifteen minutes
Cooking Time: 1 hour 52 minutes
Servings: 6
Ingredients:

1 (2-inch) piece fresh ginger, chopped

5-10 garlic cloves, chopped

1 teaspoon ground cumin

½ teaspoon ground turmeric

1 tablespoon hot paprika

1 tablespoon red pepper flakes

Salt, to taste

2 tablespoons cider vinegar

2-pounds pork shoulder, trimmed and cubed into 1½-inch size

2 cups domestic hot water, divided

1 (1-inch wide) ball tamarind pulp

¼ cup olive oil

1 teaspoon black mustard seeds, crushed

4 green cardamoms

5 whole cloves

1 (3-inch) cinnamon stick

1 cup onion, chopped finely

1 large red bell pepper, seeded and chopped

Directions:

In a food processor, add ginger, garlic, cumin, turmeric, paprika, red pepper flakes, salt and cider vinegar and pulse till smooth.

Transfer the amalgamation into a large bowl.

Add pork and coat with mixture generously.

Keep aside, covered for around an hour at room temperature.

In a bowl, add 1 cup of warm water and tamarind and make aside till water becomes cool.

With the hands, crush the tamarind to extract the pulp.

Add remaining cup of hot water and mix till well combined.

Through a fine sieve, strain the tamarind juice inside a bowl.

In a sizable skillet, heat oil on medium-high heat.

Add mustard seeds, green cardamoms, cloves and cinnamon stick and sauté for about 4 minutes.

Add onion and sauté for approximately 5 minutes.

Add pork and stir fry for approximately 6 minutes.

Stir in tamarind juice and convey with a boil.

Reduce the heat to medium-low and simmer 1½ hours.

Stir in bell pepper and cook for about 7 minutes.

Nutrition:

Calories: 435, Fat: 16g, Carbohydrates: 27g, Fiber: 3g, Protein: 39g

Grilled Spiced Turkey

Preparation Time: 5 minutes

Cooking Time: 20 minutes

Servings:4

Ingredients:

6 oz. skinless and sliced turkey breast

1 tsp. cinnamon

1 tsp. curry powder

1 tbsp. olive oil

1 tsp. nutmeg

Directions:

Whisk the oil and spices together and baste the turkey slices, coating thoroughly.

Cover and leave to marinade for as long as possible (ideally overnight).

When ready to cook, preheat the broiler to a medium-high heat and layer the turkey slices on a baking tray.

Place under the broiler for 15-20 minutes or according to package directions.

Turn occasionally.

Nutrition:

Calories 101, Protein 9 g, Carbs 6 g, Fat 11

Herby Chicken Stew

Preparation Time: 5 minutes
Cooking Time: 40 minutes
Servings:6
Ingredients:
10 oz. skinless and diced chicken breast
½ cup white rice
½ diced red onion
1 tsp. dried oregano
1 tsp. dried thyme
1 tsp. olive oil
½ cup diced eggplant
Black pepper
1 cup water
Directions:
Soak vegetables in warm water prior to use if possible.

Heat an oven-proof pot over medium-high heat and add olive oil.

Add the diced chicken breast and brown in the pot for 5-6 minutes, stirring to brown each side.

Once the chicken is browned, lower the heat to medium and add the vegetables to the pot to sauté for 5-6 minutes - careful not to let the vegetables brown.

Add the water, herbs and pepper and bring to the boil.

Reduce the heat and simmer (lid on) for 30-40 minutes or until chicken is thoroughly cooked through.

Meanwhile, prepare your rice by rinsing in cold water first and then adding to a pan of cold water and bringing to the boil over high heat.

Reduce the heat to medium and cook for 15 minutes.

Drain the rice and add back to the pan with the lid on to steam until the stew is ready.

Serve the stew on a bed of rice and enjoy!
Nutrition:
Calories 143, Protein 15 g, Carbs 9 g, Fat 5 g

Lemon & Herb Chicken Wraps

Preparation Time: 5 minutes
Cooking Time: 30 minutes
Servings:4
Ingredients:

4 oz. skinless and sliced chicken breasts

½ sliced red bell pepper

1 lemon

4 large iceberg lettuce leaves

1 tbsp. olive oil

2 tbsps. Finely chopped fresh cilantro

¼ tsp. black pepper

Directions:

Preheat the oven to 375°F/Gas Mark 5.

Mix the oil, juice of ½ lemon, cilantro and black pepper.

Marinate the chicken in the oil marinade, cover and leave in the fridge for as long as possible.

Wrap the chicken in parchment paper, drizzling over the remaining marinade.

Place in the oven in an oven dish for 25-30 minutes or until chicken is thoroughly cooked through and white inside.

Divide the sliced bell pepper and layer onto each lettuce leaf.

Divide the chicken onto each lettuce leaf and squeeze over the remaining lemon juice to taste.

Season with a little extra black pepper if desired.

Wrap and enjoy!

Nutrition:

Calories 200, Protein 9 g, Carbs 5 g, Fat 13 g

Ginger & Bean Sprout Steak Stir-Fry

Preparation Time: 4 minutes

Cooking Time: 10 minutes

Servings:2

Ingredients:

2 tsps. Grated fresh ginger

1 tsp. coconut oil

1 tsp. nutmeg

1 finely sliced green onion

¼ cup bean sprouts

5 oz. sliced lean organic beef steak

1 minced garlic clove

Directions:

Slice the beef into strips and add to a dry hot pan, cooking for 4-5 minutes on each side or until they're cooked to your liking. Set aside.

Add the oil to a clean pan and sauté the bean sprouts and onions with the ginger, garlic and nutmeg for 1 minute.

Serve the beef strips on a bed of the vegetables and enjoy.

Nutrition:

Calories 227, Protein 13 g, Carbs 13 g, Fat 23 g

Carrot & Ginger Chicken Noodles

Preparation Time: 5 minutes,
Cooking Time: 10 minutes
Servings:4
Ingredients:

1 sliced green onion

2 tsps. grated fresh ginger

4 oz. skinless sliced chicken breasts

1 lime

1 minced garlic clove

1 cup cooked rice noodles

1 tsp. coconut oil

1 peeled and grated carrot

Directions:

Heat a wok or large pan over medium-high heat.

Add the coconut oil to a pan and once melted, add the sliced chicken and brown for 4-5 minutes.

Now add the ginger and garlic and sauté for 4-5 minutes.

Add the green onion, carrot and lime juice to the wok.

Add the cooked noodles to the wok and toss until hot through.

Serve piping hot and enjoy.

Nutrition:

Calories 187, Protein 11 g, Carbs 25 g, Fat 5 g

Roast Beef

Preparation Time: 25 minutes

Cooking Time: 55 minutes

Serves:3

Ingredients:

Quality rump or sirloin tip roast

Directions:

Place in roasting pan on a shallow rack

Season with pepper and herbs

Insert meat thermometer in the center or thickest part of the roast

Roast to the desired degree of doneness

After removing from over for about 15 minutes let it chill

In the end the roast should be moister than well done.

Nutrition:

Calories 158, Protein 24 g, Fat 6 g, Carbs 0 g

Beef Brochettes

Preparation Time: 20 minutes
Cooking Time: 60 minutes
Servings:1
Ingredients:

1 ½ cups pineapple chunks

1 sliced large onion

2 lbs. thick steak

1 sliced medium bell pepper

For the marinade:

1 bay leaf

¼ cup vegetable oil

½ cup lemon juice

2 crushed garlic cloves

Directions:

Cut beef cubes and place in a plastic bag

Combine marinade ingredients in small bowl

Mix and pour over beef cubes

Seal the bag and refrigerate for 3 to 5 hours

Divide **Ingredients:** onion, beef cube, green pepper, pineapple

Grill about 9 minutes each side

Nutrition:

Calories 304, Protein 35 g, Fat 15 g, Carbs 11 g

Country Fried Steak

Preparation Time: 10 minutes
Cooking Time: 100 minutes
Servings:3
Ingredients:

1 large onion

½ cup flour

3 tbsps. vegetable oil

¼ tsp. pepper

1½ lbs. round steak

½ tsp. paprika

Directions:

Trim excess fat from steak

Cut into small pieces

Combine flour, paprika and pepper and mix together

Preheat skillet with oil

Cook steak on both sides

When the color of steak is brown remove to a platter

Add water (150 ml) and stir around the skillet

Return browned steak to skillet, if necessary, add water again so that bottom side of steak does not stick

Nutrition:

Calories 248, Protein 30 g, Fat 10 g, Carbs 5 g

Beef Pot Roast

Preparation Time: 20 minutes
Cooking Time: 60 minutes
Servings:3
Ingredients:
Round bone roast
2 - 4 lbs. chuck roast
Directions:
Trim off excess fat
Place a tablespoon of oil in a large skillet and heat to medium
Roll pot roast in flour and brown on all sides in a hot skillet
After the meat gets a brown color, reduce heat to low
Season with pepper and herbs and add ½ cup of water
Cook slowly for 1½ hours or until it looks ready
Nutrition:
Calories 157, Protein 24 g, Fat 13 g, Carbs 0 g

Meat Loaf

Preparation Time: 20 minutes
Cooking Time: 20 minutes
Servings:1
Ingredients:
½ tsp. ground sage
1 egg
¼ tsp. garlic powder
1 cup milk
1 tbsp. chopped parsley
4 soft bread slices
½ lb. lean ground pork
¼ tsp. pepper
¼ tsp. mustard
1 lb. lean ground beef
¼ cup onion
Directions:
Heat oven at 350 °F
Mix elements in a bowl

Place mixture in a shallow baking dish

Bake ½ hours or until done (At the end loaf should be crispy brown)

Nutrition:

Calories 261, Protein 27 g, Fat 12 g, Carbs 8 g

Lemon Sprouts

Preparation Time: 10 minutes
Cooking Time: 0 minutes
Serving: 4
Ingredients:
1-pound Brussels sprouts, trimmed and shredded
8 tablespoons olive oil
1 lemon, juiced and zested
Salt and pepper to taste
¾ cup spicy almond and seed mix
Directions:
Take a bowl and mix in lemon juice, salt, pepper and olive oil
Mix well
Stir in shredded Brussels sprouts and toss
Let it sit for 10 minutes
Add nuts and toss
Serve and enjoy!
Nutrition:
Calories: 382
Fat: 36g
Carbohydrates: 9g
Protein: 7g

Lemon And Broccoli Platter

Preparation Time: 10 minutes

Cooking Time: 15 minutes

Serving: 6

Ingredients:

2 heads broccoli, separated into florets

2 teaspoons extra virgin olive oil

1 teaspoon salt

½ teaspoon black pepper

1 garlic clove, minced

½ teaspoon lemon juice

Directions:

Preheat your oven to 400 °F

Take a large-sized bowl and add broccoli florets

Drizzle olive oil and season with pepper, salt, and garlic

Spread the broccoli out in a single even layer on a baking sheet

Bake for 15-20 minutes until fork tender

Squeeze lemon juice on top

Serve and enjoy!

Nutrition:

Calories: 49

Fat: 1.9g

Carbohydrates: 7g

Protein: 3g

Chicken Liver Stew

Preparation Time: 10 minutes
Cooking Time: 20 minutes
Serving: 2
Ingredients:
10 ounces chicken livers
1-ounce onion, chopped
2 ounces sour cream
1 tablespoon olive oil
Salt to taste
Directions:
Take a pan and place it over medium heat
Add oil and let it heat up
Add onions and fry until just browned
Add livers and season with salt
Cook until livers are half cooked
Transfer the mix to a stew pot
Add sour cream and cook for 20 minutes
Serve and enjoy!
Nutrition:
Calories: 146
Fat: 9g
Carbohydrates: 2g
Protein: 15g

Mushroom Cream Soup

Preparation Time: 5 minutes
Cooking Time: 30 minutes
Serving: 4
Ingredients:
1 tablespoon olive oil
½ large onion, diced
20 ounces mushrooms, sliced
6 garlic cloves, minced
2 cups vegetable broth
1 cup coconut cream
¾ teaspoon salt
¼ teaspoon black pepper
Directions:
Take a large-sized pot and place it over medium heat
Add onion and mushrooms in olive oil and Sauté for 10-15 minutes
Make sure to keep stirring it from time to time until browned evenly
Add garlic and Sauté for 10 minutes more
Add vegetable broth, coconut cream, coconut milk, black pepper, and salt
Bring it to a boil and reduce the temperature to low
Simmer for 15 minutes
Use an immersion blender to puree the mixture
Enjoy!
Nutrition:
Calories: 200
Fat: 17g
Carbohydrates: 5g
Protein: 4g

Garlic Soup

Preparation Time: 10 minutes
Cooking Time: 60 minutes
Serving: 10
Ingredients:
1 tablespoon olive oil
2 bulbs garlic, peeled
3 shallots, chopped
1 large head cauliflower, chopped
6 cups vegetable broth
Salt and pepper to taste
Directions:
Preheat your oven to 400 °F
Slice ¼ inch top off the garlic bulb and place it in aluminum foil
Grease with olive oil and roast in the oven for 35 minutes
Squeeze the flesh out of the roasted garlic
Heat oil in a saucepan and add shallots, Sautė for 6 minutes
Add the garlic and remaining ingredients
Cover the pan and reduce the heat to low
Let it cook for 15-20 minutes
Use an immersion blender to puree the mixture
Season soup with salt and pepper
Serve and enjoy!
Nutrition:
Calories: 142
Fat: 8g
Carbohydrates: 3.4g
Protein: 4g

Conclusion

Thank you for sticking with us all the way to the end! We hope we were able to set you on the right path to selecting and preparing a delicious meal to help with improving the health of your kidneys. These Renal Diet recipes are perfect to share with the whole family.

Keep practicing and exploring new and exciting meals from this book. Mix and match the delicious recipes presented, to come up with your new favorite Renal Diet meal then share them with your friends, and family!

I encourage you to return to this guidebook any time you are in doubt or you whenever you would like to get back to useful tips on how to live a healthier life with damaged renal functions and chronic kidney disease. The state of your renal function is what defines how well your organism and your body are functioning, however, as explained in the book, your health should see crucial improvements with the change of your everyday diet.

Make sure to always check your labels when shopping for groceries and take care that the meals you are preparing are made ready in accordance with the low-potassium and low-sodium diet for best results and remember that healthy habits make a healthy life.

Enjoy your journey to a more quality life and balanced renal health!